STAMPS
THE BEGINNING COLLECTOR

GARY DUNAIER

MALLARD
PRESS

An imprint of
BDD Promotional Book Company, Inc.
666 Fifth Avenue
New York, New York 10103

A FRIEDMAN GROUP BOOK

Published by MALLARD PRESS
An imprint of BDD Promotional Book Company, Inc.
666 Fifth Avenue
New York, New York 10103

Mallard Press and its accompanying design and logo are trademarks of
BDD Promotional Book Company, Inc.

Copyright © 1992 by Michael Friedman Publishing Group, Inc.

First published in the United States of America in 1992 by The Mallard Press

ISBN 0-792-45474-X

THE BEGINNING COLLECTOR: STAMPS
was prepared and produced by
Michael Friedman Publishing Group, Inc.
15 West 26th Street
New York, NY 10010

Editor: Stephen Williams
Design and Layout: William Sponn
Photography Editor: Ede Rothaus
Photographs by: John Gruen, New York
Illustrative material courtesy of Lee Rosenbloom

The stamps photographed in this book are from the stamp collection and inventory
of Regal Galleries, Inc. Anyone interested in obtaining any of these stamps or
having questions regarding stamps in general may write Regal Galleries, Inc.,
101 West 57th Street, New York, New York 10019.

Typeset by: Classic Type, Inc.
Color separations by: Excel Graphic Arts Company
Printed and bound in Hong Kong by: Lee Fung-Asco Printer Ltd.

Dedication

I hereby dedicate this book to two people: Sol Koved and Martin Band.

Sol Koved was the editor of *First Days*—the official journal of the American First Day Cover Society—from 1960 to 1990. By publishing my articles in *First Days,* he gave me access to the wonderful world of writing about stamps. His encouragement and support of my work was invaluable.

Martin Band, a stamp dealer I used to work for. One day Mr. Band told me he had a ticket to a stamp show that he wasn't going to use and asked if I would like to use it. I went to the show, and a temporarily dormant interest in stamp collecting was rekindled.

I'd also like to thank my editor, Stephen Williams. I enjoy writing —it's something that comes very easily to me. But putting words on paper and getting everything organized into book form are two completely different issues. That's where Stephen came in.

CONTENTS

Introduction

You want to know how to acquire stamps, so let's not waste any time. Here's how:

Step 1: Go to the post office and buy some stamps.

Step 2: Go home and take the stamps off your mail.

Step 3: Ask your friends, family, and coworkers if they have any stamps to give you.

Step 4: Put your stamps in a box.

That's it. Now you know all about how to *accumulate* stamps. But there's a *big* difference between accumulating stamps, and being a true collector. Once you've finished this book, you'll know how to *collect* stamps.

What's the difference between accumulating and collecting? An accumulator acquires objects just for the sake of it. It doesn't matter what they are—for an accumulator, stamps may just be one element of a large and assorted collection of stuff. The so-called stamp collection that belongs to an accumulator may in reality be nothing more than randomly acquired stamps, arranged in no discernible order. An accumulator's goal may be to just get, say, a million stamps for as little money as possible. This is not all that difficult to do, especially if one is willing to accept duplicates (an accumulator would be willing), because there are plenty of stamps that can be obtained cheaply, especially in quantity.

HOW COLLECTORS LOOK AT STAMPS

The collector is different. Collectors study their stamps and learn the history behind each. Why was it issued?

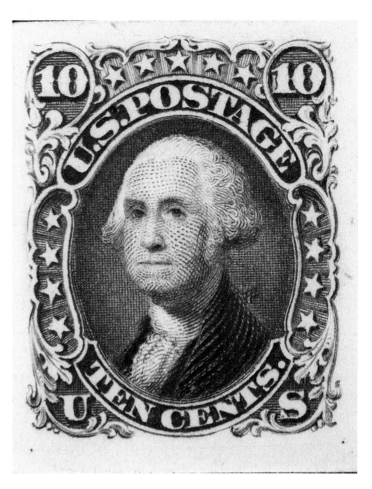

This 10¢ stamp depicting George Washington was issued in 1861.

Why did this person or that event merit commemoration? What was the postal rate at the time this stamp was issued?

The collector learns that some stamps with the same design and face value were issued in different formats, including sheets, coils (rolls), and booklets. The collector learns that some stamps are valid only in conjunction with certain postal services. The collector learns that other stamps, issued with the intention of meeting a particular rate or paying for a special service, are actually valid on all kinds of mail.

The collector learns all of this, and much more. The accumulator doesn't—in fact, the accumulator doesn't care. Accumulators will find this book of little or no interest, because unlike you, they just want to accumulate, not collect. But believe me, you'll find that collecting stamps is much more fun than accumulating them.

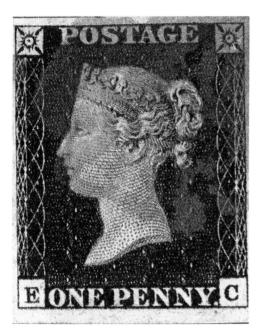

The "Penny Black," issued May 1840 in Great Britain, was the world's first postage stamp. (It got its nickname from its face value—one penny—and its color, black.) The portrait of Queen Victoria that appears on the stamp was taken from a commemorative medal issued three years earlier. The "E" and "C" on the bottom are part of a security measure designed to prevent counterfeiting, with the letters indicating that stamp's exact position in the sheet. This stamp was in the fifth row from the top ("E"), third from the left ("C"). The Penny Black doesn't actually say it's from Great Britain, primarily because, as the first postage stamp in the world, there wasn't any need to identify its issuer.

So what *is* a postage stamp? Some people will tell you it's a miniature work of art. Others will say it's a little bit of history. Still others will even go so far as to say stamps are wonderful investments. But when you get right down to it, a postage stamp is just a receipt—a label telling the postal service that you've paid the fee to have your letter transported from point A to point B.

THE HISTORY OF STAMPS

Today, you wouldn't even think of mailing a letter without putting a stamp on it. But in the days before stamps, not only did people not put stamps on their mail, but often it was the *recipient*, not the sender, who paid the postage! That's right, the sender had the option of paying postage. Because of this, delivery was never guaranteed—just as you don't have to accept a collect telephone call, the recipient did not have to accept the letter. In the United States this ended in 1856, when prepayment of letters was made compulsory.

Stamps have had a long and colorful history. The first postage stamp was issued in Great Britain in 1840. Before postage stamps came along, people brought their letters to the post office, and if they were willing to prepay the postage, the postmaster would either write a notation or use a handstamp to indicate the postage was paid. Envelopes are known to collectors as covers, and these types are known as stampless covers because they don't bear adhesive stamps.

Great Britain was the first country to issue stamps (it issued the Penny Black, the first stamp, in 1840), so it has the honor of not having to put the country's name on its stamps. This is an exception to the regulations of the Universal Postal Union (UPU), which require all nations to put the name of their country on their stamps. Interestingly, the United States has violated this rule several times. In 1920, a set of stamps commemorating the three-hundredth anniversary of the Pilgrims' landing at Plym-

outh Rock did not mention the United States anywhere, and in 1963, a 5¢ regular issue also did not—although this stamp, depicting the White House and the American flag, had enough Americana that it couldn't be mistaken as anything other than a United States stamp.

Another interesting UPU regulation is that for a stamp to be valid on international mail, it has to have a figure of value printed on it. This is why United States stamps issued just after a rate change with letters on them in place of a value are inscribed "Domestic Mail." You can't use them on mail bound overseas.

The first United States stamps were issued in 1847, but they weren't the first postage stamps issued in America.

This U.S. stamp violates the UPU rule. It does not say which country issued it—at least, not in words. However, there are plenty of design elements that clearly identify this as a U.S. stamp—specifically, the large flag, and the White House. It's a 1963 five cent definitive that saw plenty of use in its day.

_1837_

Geo. Schock, Esq

Womelsdorf

_Pa_

LOUISVILLE
MAY
20
KY.

Back in the days before stamps, this is what the mail looked like. Today these kinds of envelopes are known as "stampless covers." You'd present your letter to the window clerk, pay the postage (whcih in those days was based on distance as well as weight), and the letter would be postmarked and the indication of the postage paid was either handwritten or handstamped. This cover is from 1837, and was mailed in Louisville, Kentucky. The address is given only as name and city: Back then mail was only delivered from post office to post office.

Some individual postmasters decided to issue their own stamps, which would be valid in their own cities and post offices. Today, these stamps are known as postmasters' provisionals and are very collectible. Postmasters' provisionals were legitimate stamps, except that they were valid only in the area under the jurisdiction of the postmaster issuing them. In the eyes of postal clerks, they were indicators that postage was paid, just as much as a handstamp or manuscript marking.

The first stamps were issued _imperforate_—that is, without perforations. Stamps had to be cut apart with scissors, and today copies of classic early stamps with wide margins on all four sides are especially prized, because it was quite easy to cut into the design. The United States started issuing perforated stamps in 1857. Some stamps were issued in both perforate and imperforate versions, and on these stamps you should be careful to make sure that the imperforate stamp you're buying really _is_ imperforate, and not just a trimmed perforated stamp.

One interesting thing about American stamps is that to this day all but the earliest issues are still valid for post-

A typical used 1861 three cent U.S. stamp, with the cancellation obliterating most of the stamp. As a used stamp it's actually quite common and inexpensive.

age. In 1861, at the outbreak of the Civil War, the earlier issues were declared invalid in order to prevent post offices in the South from using them. Of course, you wouldn't *want* to use a stamp from 1861 for postage today, because mint examples are worth far more than the first-class letter rate, but it's nice to know that you *could* if you wanted to.

The honor of which country issued the very first commemorative postal item is in dispute, but one of the candidates for the distinction is the United States, which, in 1876, issued a 3¢ prestamped envelope commemorating the nation's centennial. (This design was reissued for the bicentennial, in 1976, in a 13¢ denomination to meet the then-current rates.) The United States' first commemorative adhesive stamps were issued in 1893—a sixteen-stamp set with values ranging from 1¢ to $5 to commemorate the four-hundredth anniversary of the discovery of America by Christopher Columbus and the World Columbian Exposition in Chicago. The total face value for the set was $16.34, which in those days represented a *lot* of money to the average citizen, when the

typical salary was just a few dollars a week.

Stamp production was originally contracted out to private security printers. In 1894, however, the government's Bureau of Engraving and Printing (BEP), the printers of United States currency, took over production of the nation's postage stamps as well. Today, stamps are produced by both the BEP and private companies. There's plenty of work to go around. (Some collectors say there's *too much* postal product coming out these days, but that's a separate issue.)

The first airmail stamp was issued in 1918, a two-color stamp depicting an airplane. One hundred of these stamps mistakenly were printed with the plane upside down, making them especially collectible. In 1926, the United States' first souvenir sheet was produced—a sheet of twenty-five (as opposed to the customary one hundred) of a commemorative, with a special inscription in the selvage. In 1975, America's first nondenominated stamps were issued.

Only a few of the many events in the 150-year-plus history of stamps have been mentioned here. And the history of postage stamps is not a closed book: Postal services around the world are continually trying to find new ways to issue stamps in order to meet customers' demands. Other innovations include a prestamped envelope issued by the United States with the design in a hologram; self-adhesive stamps; and *plastic* stamps designed to be sold through bank automated teller machines (ATMs). Perhaps one day in the future, hologram stamps, EXTRAordinary cards, self-adhesive stamps, and ATM-vended stamps will be commonplace, just as Express Mail and fax service is to us today. Times are changing, and stamps reflect the times.

A booklet pane of six one-cent stamps from 1907 (opposite). The United States first issued stamps in booklet form in 1900, and they sold for one cent above face value until the 1960s. Booklets are very popular with today's postal customers, and a number of commemoratives have been issued exclusively in booklet format since 1986.

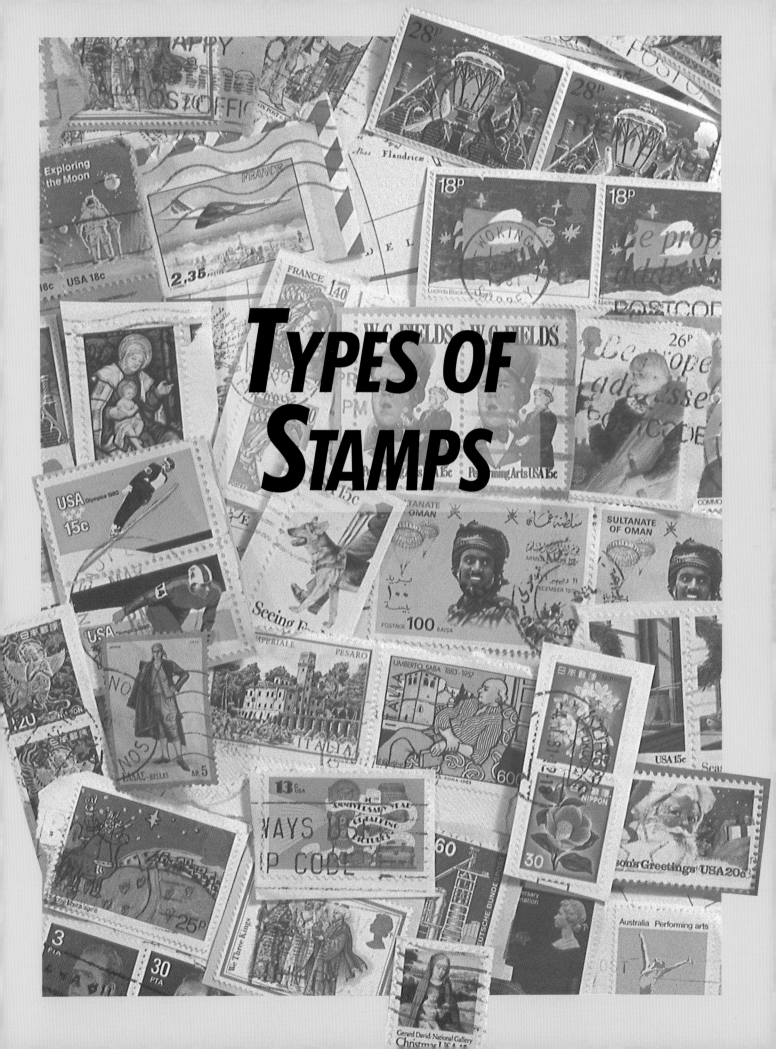

TYPES OF STAMPS

Through the years the U.S. has issued many stamps intended exclusively to pay particular fees above and beyond the cost of postage (certified mail, special delivery, etc.). This is the only stamp the U.S. has ever issued for registered mail. It was issued in 1911.

1840: The world's first postage stamp, the Penny Black, is issued, in England. Since it was the only country issuing stamps, Great Britain left off the name of the country—a practice it continues to this day.

When people go to the post office to buy stamps, they usually just ask for a book, a roll, or a sheet of stamps, or they tell the window clerk how many stamps they want. Customers might sometimes ask for a commemorative that is advertised on the post office wall. But for the most part, people take what they're given.

But you, as a collector, will encounter different kinds of stamps. What kinds of stamps are there? Collectors categorize stamps by type, function, and the way they are issued. These are all important to understand.

There are two different types of stamps. *Commemoratives,* as you might guess, are stamps that commemorate a person or an event. They're sold only for six months to a

The "A" stamp of 1978, issued when the letter rate was raised from thirteen cents to fifteen cents. The U.S. prepares nondenominated stamps such as these far ahead of time to ensure a plentiful supply without having to commit to a value before a new rate receives approval from the Postal Rate Commission. Although the fifteen cent letter rate has long since passed, this stamp will always be worth fifteen cents towards the cost of postage. However, because the value is not stated but merely indicated, nondenominated stamps can only be used on mail within the U.S. (A Canadian postal clerk isn't going to know what "A" is worth—in fact, Canada issued their own "A" stamps in 1981, face value 30 cents Canadian—those stamps can only be used on letters within Canada.)

year. *Definitives* are the workhorses of the post office. They're what you see on your mail most frequently. They're smaller than commemoratives, and they're kept on sale for a longer period of time than commemoratives. Unlike commemoratives, definitives usually do not honor a particular event.

FUNCTIONS OF STAMPS

All stamps are issued to serve a particular function. Most commemoratives are issued to meet the current first-class letter rate. In 1986, the rate in the United States was 22¢, so the commemoratives issued that year had a face value of 22¢. In 1990, it cost 25¢ to mail a letter, so the commemoratives issued in 1990 had a face

This 1913 United States Parcel Post stamp was the very first stamp issued by any nation to show an airplane. The use of airplanes to carry mail has become so widespread that the fee for domestic airmail has been eliminated. The only airmail items the U.S. issues these days (such as this postal card, issued in December 1979 as publicity for the 1980 Moscow Olympics) are to meet international airmail rates.

value of a quarter, and so on.

There have also been stamps for *airmail* service. The first airmail stamp in the world was issued in the United States in 1918. A separate airmail rate for domestic letters was eliminated in 1977, because most domestic letters that needed it were transported by air anyway. Airmail stamps are still issued for international mail.

A second cousin to airmail stamps are *Express Mail* stamps, which were first issued in 1983. Express Mail stamps are intended for packages that will be sent by Express Mail, although they can be used on any kind of mailable matter. They are the highest-denomination stamps ever issued by the United States Postal Service.

A *Priority Mail* stamp with a face value $2.40 was issued in 1989. Although this stamp is not a commemora-

These Express Mail stamps are among the highest face value postage stamps the U.S. has issued. Although they were issued specifically to meet the Express Mail rates, they're good on other kinds of mail as well. The designs are evocative of the Express Mail advertising campaigns the Postal Service was using at the time these stamps were issued. The $10.75 stamp, top, was issued in 1985 and covered Express Mail packages weighing two pounds or less; the $8.75 value, bottom, came out in 1988 when a reduced rate for smaller Express Mail packages was instituted.

tive, the design commemorates the twentieth anniversary of man's landing on the moon and was issued twenty years to the day later. This stamp can be used for packages that weigh more than twelve ounces. Like Express Mail stamps, Priority Mail stamps may be used on any letters or packages for which the total amount of postage needed meets or exceeds $2.40 (naturally, you have to buy additional stamps to cover the excess).

As we've mentioned, these stamps can be used on any and all kinds of mail, although they were issued to meet particular rates. This wasn't always the case. When there was domestic airmail service, if an airmail stamp was used the letter *had* to be sent airmail. The letter would be assessed "postage-due" if there wasn't enough airmail postage, even if the letter was just going across town and

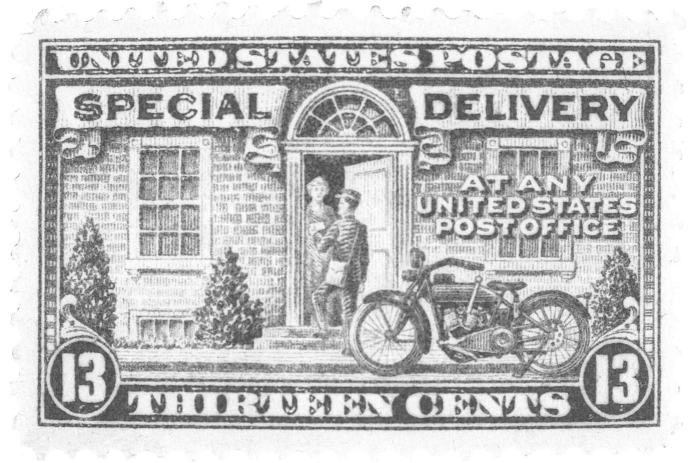

The design of this 1944 thirteen cent special delivery stamp was first used in 1922 on a ten cent special delivery stamp. It's a good example of the lost art of fine engraving. The last special delivery stamp was issued in 1971 and had a simple ''modern art'' design of two arrows pointing in opposite directions.

there was enough postage to cover the surface rate. Today, although airmail stamps still say ''Airmail'' on them, they can be used for other kinds of postage as well. Express Mail and Priority Mail stamps do not say ''Express Mail'' or ''Priority Mail'' on them, and they can be used on any kind of mail.

CROSSING THE CANADIAN BORDER

For many years Canadians have had a separate rate for letters to the United States, higher than that charged for domestic mail sent within the provinces. But the United States didn't establish such a system until 1988. It applies to Mexico as well as Canada.

Other postal services for which special stamps have been or still are issued are *special delivery* (the last such stamp was issued in 1971), *certified mail* (only one stamp, 1955) and *registration* (only one stamp for this, as well, in 1911) and parcel post. A number of parcel post stamps were issued, as well as parcel-post postage-due stamps, in 1912 and 1913. Parcel post stamps were unpopular with postal workers because they were all the same color, which made it difficult to tell which denomination was which. They were eventually declared acceptable for use on first-class mail, perhaps in an attempt to get rid of them. Stamps are also issued for the exclusive use of government agencies. They are called *official stamps,* and the general public is not allowed to use them on letters.

One kind of stamp that some countries have issued is a

This airmail special delivery stamp, issued in 1936, provided for the payment of airmail postage (six cents) and the special delivery fee (ten cents) with a single stamp. This is the second of two such stamps issued by the U.S.; the first, issued in 1934, used the same design as this one except that it was a single color: dark blue.

semipostal stamp. This is a stamp that sells for a price above and beyond the face value of the stamp, with the additional amount going to charity. Semipostal stamps have the value expressed as, for example, "25¢ + 5¢." In this case, the 25¢ would be for postage, the 5¢ would be for charity, and the selling price would be 30¢.

CANADIAN SEMI-POSTAL STAMPS

Between 1974 and 1976, Canada issued twelve semipostal stamps to help raise money for the 1976 Olympic Games, which were held in Montreal, Quebec. The charity in this case was the Canadian Olympic Committee.

The stamp sold for 10 cents—8 cents for postage, and 2 cents went for the Olympics. Some postal administrations have found that this is not necessarily a good way to raise money for charity—England issued a semipostal in 1975 and found the bookkeeping to be so complicated that it wasn't worth it to issue more, and the United States has said that because of administrative headaches such as these, they have no intention of issuing semipostal stamps. Some countries have found that semipostal stamps do not end up raising much for charity.

HOW STAMPS ARE ISSUED

Stamps are issued in many different formats. There's the *sheet* format, of course, and there's *coil,* in which the stamps are issued in a roll. Coil stamps are perforated on two sides only, usually on the left and right sides, and they're generally collected in pairs.

Stamps are also issued in *booklets,* which are convenient to carry around in wallets and purses. A page of stamps from a booklet is called a pane, and a complete booklet with all the stamps and any other pages that might have come with the booklet is referred to as an unexploded booklet. Stamps from booklets have either

These stamps are coil stamps—issued in rolls. Stamps issued in coils have two straight edges parallel with each other, and they're commonly saved in multiples of two or more to establish their status as coils. The stamps on top were issued in 1983 for the exclusive use of authorized U.S. government agencies. If you ever receive a letter with this kind of stamp on it, regardless of the face value of the stamp, save the entire envelope as such items are not commonly found. The bottom stamp was issued in 1985 and met the first class presort letter rate.

Above and left: *The United States' first postage stamps—a five-cent value showing Benjamin Franklin (shown as a used pair; note that the early stamps were issued without perforations), and a ten-cent stamp showing George Washington. Both were issued in 1847 and bear cancellations contemporary to the era. These stamps were reprinted in 1947 on a souvenir sheet celebrating the one-hundredth anniversary of the first postage stamp (page 90). Ironically, the 1947 reprints are still good for postage, but the 1847 originals aren't.*

one, two, or three straight edges—but unlike coils, they can be collected as single stamps. Some stamps are issued *only* in booklet format.

One format the Postal Service is experimenting with is *self-adhesive.* Just peel the stamps from their backing, and stick them on your letters—you don't have to wet them. A self-adhesive stamp was first issued in 1974, but it wasn't until fifteen years later that the Postal Service continued experimenting with the format. In 1989, a booklet of eighteen stamps for $5 (as opposed to twenty regular stamps that you have to lick for that price) was issued on a trial basis in fifteen different cities (which were selected for their different climates) to see how the stamps would hold up in varying temperatures. Although these stamps were sold only in a few cities, they're good for postage anywhere in the United States.

Another format collectors like is the *souvenir sheet.* That's a small sheet of one or more stamps, with a commemorative inscription or special artwork in the areas surrounding the stamp or stamps. The most recent souvenir sheets issued by the United States came out in 1989, when three sheets, each containing four stamps, were issued in honor of the Twentieth Universal Postal Congress (a gathering of postal officials from all over the world) and World Stamp Expo (a stamp show and exhibition sponsored by the United States Postal Service, and held at the Postal Congress).

There are other forms of indicia of prepayment of postage. There's *postal stationery,* which encompasses prestamped envelopes, aerogrammes (letter sheets for foreign postage), and postal cards (not to be confused with picture postcards), all of which are sold by the post office.

Postage meters are actually not stamps, but legal substitutes for them. Meters are used primarily by businesses, and the advantages to them are that they can punch up exactly the amount of postage they need (instead of, say, using two 25¢ stamps to meet a 45¢ rate because 25¢ stamps are all the company has). They prevent employees

1847: The United States issues its first postage stamps, a 5¢ stamp showing Benjamin Franklin and a 10¢ stamp depicting George Washington.

from taking stamps home. A meter renter (meters are not owned by the businesses who use them) may have postage added by bringing the machine to a post office, or, for an additional fee, a postal employee will go to the company and set the meter on the renter's premises.

Finally, there are *permit imprints,* which are available for all classes of mail. To mail using a permit, you must establish a deposit account with the Postal Service for the purpose of mailing with a permit, and you must mail more than two hundred pieces or fifty pounds at one time.

HOW STAMPS ARE PRINTED

There are many different printing methods that are used to actually manufacture stamps. Here is a brief rundown of some of them.

Engraving (also known as intaglio) is the most detailed of the procedures. Currency is also produced in this manner. A photographic reduction of the stamp's original artwork is made into a master die, a small piece of metal on which a mirror image of the design is engraved. From there a transfer roll, which transfers the design from the master die to the printing plate, is created. The finished transfer roll, which has a nonreversed image of the stamp design, transfers the image to the plate. The image is again reversed on the plate, so that when the stamps themselves are printed, they will have the correct image. On engraved stamps, the design is cut underneath the surface of the printing plate. Ink goes in the cuts, and the plate is wiped clean for each printing impression, so that only the ink inside the plate cuts prints the design. When printed, an engraved stamp has raised ink.

Typography (also known as letterpress, or surface printing) is in some ways the opposite of engraving. After the master die is made, the area that will *not* be used as a printing surface is cut away. Unlike engraving, here the ink stays on the raised, or uncut, sections of the plate.

1856: Prepayment of postage becomes mandatory. Before this time, the sender could send mail without postage, and the addressee would have to pay (if the recipient didn't want to pay, they wouldn't get their letter).

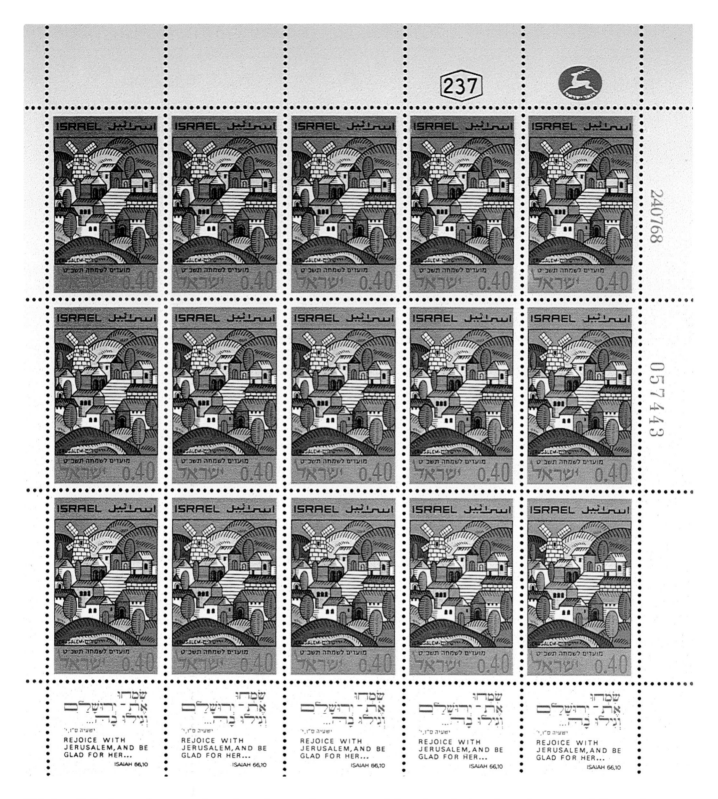

This is a full sheet of stamps from Israel, complete with plate numbers and tabs. Tabs, a popular aspect of Israeli stamps, are parts of the selvage with an inscription that gives more information about the subject being honored.

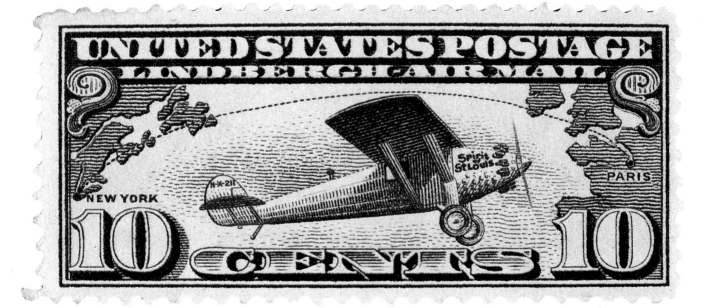

50th Anniversary Solo Transatlantic Flight

The original die is reproduced either by stereotyping or electrotyping, and then the printing plate is made.

Photogravure (also known as rotogravure) is similar to photography. The image is transferred to a special metal plate. The design is photographically transferred into many tiny dots, which on the plate are impressed in various depths, depending on the intensity of the shade needed. It is these impressions that hold the ink, and in this regard the process is similar to engraving.

Lithography is a process based on the fact that oil and water do not mix. The design of the stamp is created on a printing plate using an oily material. In this method, the parts of the printing plate that won't be printed have water on them—and since oil and water do not mix, the ink will be forced to the oily parts of the plate.

SO, YOU WANT TO BE ON A STAMP?

It's quite easy to be on a stamp. Different countries have different rules. Here are the rules for the United States. First you have to be dead—for at least ten years. That's the rule—unless you've been president, in which case you only have to be dead for one year. Other rules and guidelines have been set by the Postal Service and the Citizens' Stamp Advisory Committee (CSAC), a group that helps to determine what will be on stamps. The postmaster general has the final say on what subjects are honored with a stamp. Although most of the CSAC's recommendations are adopted, the committee's function is completely advisory. Once in a while, the postmaster general decides to issue a stamp the CSAC has no knowledge of. Anyway, here are the rules:

1. United States postage stamps should generally feature American and related subjects.

2. No living people can be honored on United States postage. But there have been exceptions. In 1927, after Charles Lindbergh made his successful New York-to-

This 1927 airmail stamp (opposite, top), issued to commemorate Charles Lindbergh's solo flight from New York to Paris, violated a postal rule which prohibits the honoring of living people on U.S. stamps—Lindbergh is mentioned by name. When a commemorative stamp was issued in 1977 on the fiftieth anniversary of that flight (opposite, bottom), Lindbergh's name was nowhere to be found. Ironically, Linbergh died in 1974, so the 1977 stamp should have mentioned him. Both stamps picture his plane, the ''Spirit of St. Louis.''

Paris solo flight, the United States issued airmail stamps showing Lindbergh's plane, the *Spirit of St. Louis*, and the stamp bore the aviator's name. (Ironically, when the fiftieth anniversary of the flight was postally commemorated in 1977, the stamp had a picture of the plane, but only mentioned the flight anniversary—Lindbergh wasn't mentioned, even though he was deceased.) And in 1969, an airmail stamp commemorating the first man on the moon showed an astronaut stepping onto the surface of the moon. Obviously, this was Neil Armstrong, though he is not mentioned on the stamp because he was living when it was introduced.

3. Stamps honoring individuals are usually issued on, or in conjunction with, significant anniversaries of their birth. But, as already stated, no postal item can be issued sooner than ten years after the honoree's death—except for American presidents, who are honored with a memorial stamp on the first birthday after their death.

4. Significant events are commemorated only on anniversaries in multiples of fifty years.

5. Only those events and anniversaries of widespread national importance are considered for commemoration. Locally or regionally significant events may be honored with a special cancellation (the printed "stamp" the post office marks across your stamps to cancel them), which can be arranged through the local postmaster.

6. Stamps are not issued to honor fraternal, political, sectarian, or service organizations whose main reason for being is to solicit or distribute funds. Neither are stamps issued to honor commercial enterprises or specific products. (That means there cannot be stamps for McDonald's or Coca-Cola, for example.)

7. Stamps cannot be issued to honor cities, towns, schools, hospitals, libraries, or similar institutions. There are just so many of them that it would be difficult to single out individuals. However, there are ways to get around this rule—for example, in 1986 a stamp was issued saluting public hospitals. It was issued in New York, and the

1857: The United States begins perforating its stamps.

Two of the sixteen stamps issued in 1893 to honor the World's Columbian Exposition, a Chicago fair which celebrated the four hundredth anniversary of the discovery of America by Christopher Columbus. These are among the first commemorative stamps issued by any government.

site of the dedication ceremony was held in New York's Bellevue Hospital—which, coincidentally, just happened to be celebrating its 250th anniversary that year.

8. Observances of statehood are made only at intervals of fifty years from the date the state became part of the United States. State-related or regional anniversaries are considered for postal stationery (postal cards or envelopes)—and again, only at intervals of fifty years.

9. Stamps cannot be issued to honor religious institutions or people who are primarily associated with religious activities or beliefs.

10. Semipostals cannot be issued. Government policy states that it's unfair to single out one charity for this purpose. In addition, administrative costs would eat into any moneys raised for charity. In 1975, Great Britain issued a semipostal stamp, and the sales results were so disastrous that they haven't issued one since.

11. Significant anniversaries of universities and other institutions of higher learning can only be commemorated on "Historic Preservation" postal cards, and if such a card is issued, the design must show an appropriate building on the campus.

These guidelines were first created in 1957, and they've been gradually expanded on ever since. If you have an idea for a possible subject for a postage stamp, and it falls within these parameters, send your idea to this address: Citizens' Stamp Advisory Committee, Stamp Information Branch, United States Postal Service, Washington, DC 20260–6352. A lot of lead time is needed for design and production, so you should only suggest subjects suitable for commemorating a minimum of three years from now.

1873: Postal cards make their debut in the United States. Not to be confused with a picture postcard, a *postal card* is a card you buy at the post office with the stamp already printed. A picture postcard is a privately printed card with a photograph or illustration on one side and the message and address area on the other; you have to put a stamp on it in order to mail it.

BILINGUAL STAMPS

Some stamps are bilingual. Canadian stamps, for example, are inscribed in both English and French, as required under Canadian law.

Sometimes Canada's bilingualism is nothing more than a simple "Postage/Postes," but there have been issues saluting Securitie Routiere (Highway Safety, 1966), La Legion Royale Canadienne (The Royal Canadian Legion, 1975), and Code Postal (Postal Code—a series of letters and numbers that make up Canada's equivalent of the American Zip code, 1979). There are even stamps for when someone mails a letter that's A Percevoir (Postage Due).

Collectors on Canada Post's mailing list receive colorful brochures, printed in English and French, that describe upcoming issues. You can get on its mailing list by sending a request to the Canadian Post Office. Its address is in the back of the book, along with the addresses of many other foreign postal administrations—for the day when

Commemorative postal items are not restricted to adhesive stamps, as demonstrated by this 1974 aerogramme (letter sheet for foreign postage) honoring the twenty-fifth anniversary of NATO, and a 1974 international airmail postal card with the message "Visit USA— Bicentennial Era."

Shown above is a stamp issued by the postmaster of New York City in 1845, two years before the first U.S. stamps were issued. Prior to 1847, some local postmasters issued their own stamps, which were valid only in the city where issued; such stamps are known as ''postmasters' provisionals'' and are highly collectible today. The New York postmasters' provisionals were usually initialed in magenta for control purposes before they were sold; the blue lines are pen strokes, a typical form of cancellation for the day.

you feel confident enough to test your language skills on a country that doesn't put *any* English on its stamps!

UNITED STATES-CANADA JOINT ISSUES

The United States and Canada share a common border. They've also shared a number of joint issues. A joint issue is a stamp that two or more countries issue at or about the same time, on the same topic. Sometimes the designs are alike, sometimes not.

In 1959, stamps were issued commemorating the opening of the St. Lawrence Seaway. In 1976, stamps honoring Benjamin Franklin were issued. Both times, the two countries shared the same design. In 1977, stamps were issued to celebrate the opening of the Peace Bridge, connecting Fort Erie, Ontario with Buffalo, New York. These designs were completely different. And just to make matters interesting, in 1984 the twenty-fifth anniversary of the same St. Lawrence Seaway was the subject of another joint issue—but while the designs were basically similar, the sizes of the stamps weren't, with Canada issuing a longer stamp.

The United States has also issued stamps in connection with Australia, the Netherlands, and even the Soviet Union! Collecting joint issues is a fun sideline that many collectors enjoy.

Getting Started

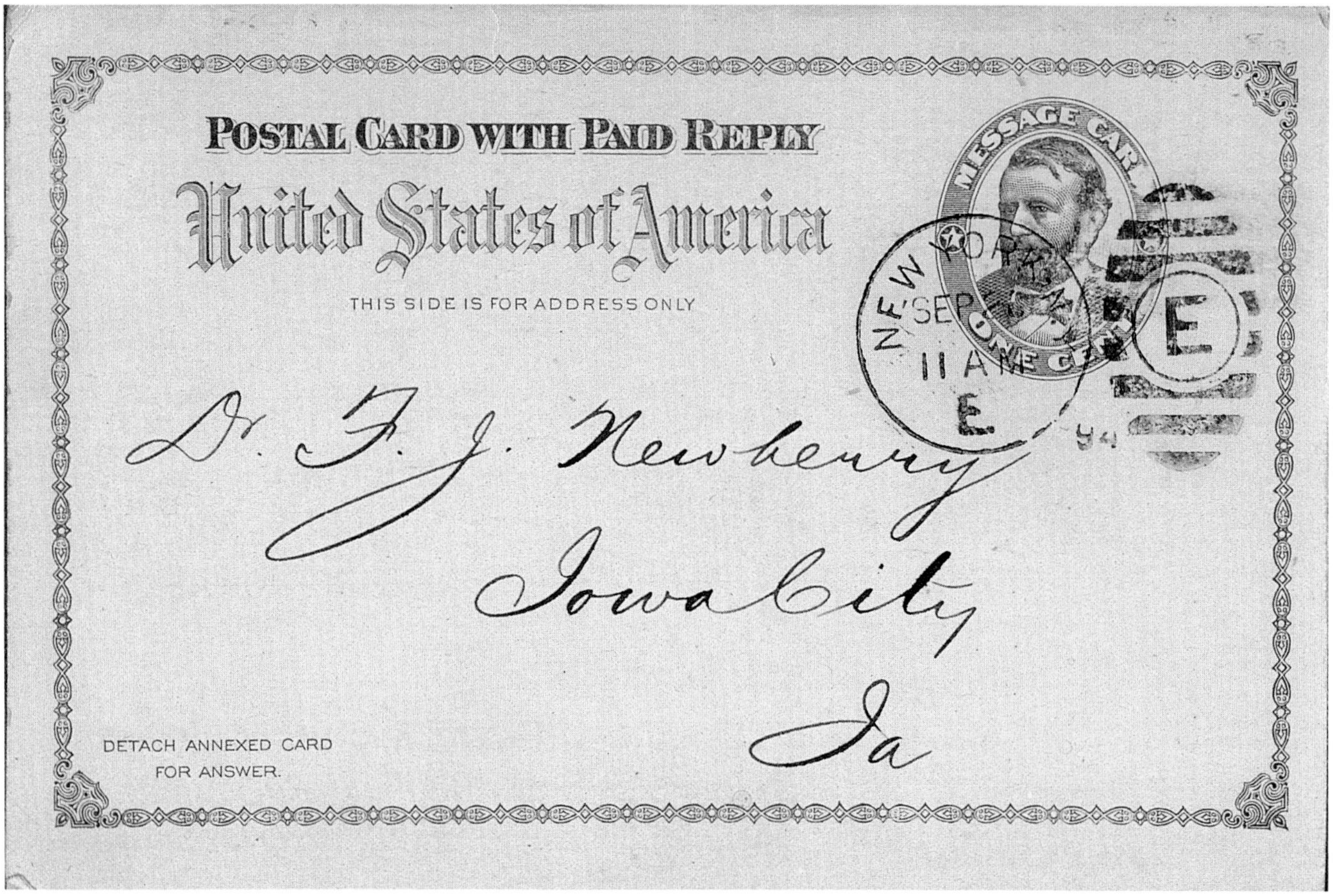

POSTAL CARD WITH PAID REPLY
United States of America
THIS SIDE IS FOR ADDRESS ONLY
MESSAGE CARD
ONE CENT
NEW YORK
SEP
11 AM
E
94
E
Dr. F. J. Newberry
Iowa City
Ia
DETACH ANNEXED CARD
FOR ANSWER.

This "postal card with paid reply" pictures president Ulysses S. Grant and was issued in 1892. A paid reply postal card is the postal card equivalent of a self-addressed stamped envelope—they're sold as two attached cards, one for the message and the other for the reply.

The best way to begin collecting is to get as many stamps as you can. Yes, that *is* accumulating, and yes, the goal *is* to get you to be a collector, not an accumulator. However, five or ten years down the road, you won't be buying stamps in a haphazard manner, unless, of course, you *choose* to collect this way. In any event, you have to actually *see* stamps—in front of you, not in pictures in a catalog—in order to discover what you like.

Why are you reading this book? Because you want to know how to collect stamps. And why do you want to collect stamps? You must see something in stamps that appeals to you to make you want to collect them. Unfortunately, it's impossible to collect one of everything, so you'll have to specialize. But before you can specialize, you have to know what's out there, and *that's* why you should acquire as many different stamps as you can.

The Basics

One very valuable piece of advice: *don't* spend all of your stamp-collecting money on stamps. You should also buy some philatelic literature such as catalogs and periodicals. More than anything, it's *knowledge* that separates the accumulator from the collector. Literature will be discussed more fully in the next chapter, but the importance of buying books about stamps in addition to buying stamps themselves should be stressed. The Postal Service publishes an annual paperback, *The Postal Service Guide to U.S. Stamps*, which is sold at most post offices. With color photographs of every American stamp from the first one, issued in 1847, it's like a miniature collection of stamps that gets updated every year. The book costs $6, and for that price, you can't afford *not* to have it.

This is the other half of the card shown on page 38. Note the inscription ''Reply postal card'' on top, otherwise the cards are the same. The address is printed, indicating that these cards were used as a sort of form letter.

Mixtures and Packets

Stamp dealers, naturally, can sell you stamps, and we'll discuss dealers in a little more detail later on—but you're at an early stage in your collection, so one stamp is pretty much the same as another. Hence, one of the best ways to acquire a lot of stamps quickly is to buy *mixtures* or *packets.*

Mixtures are stamps sold in large quantities, even by the thousands. They're also sold by weight. You can buy them either on paper or off paper. *On paper* means that the stamps come with part of the envelope. *Off paper* means the stamps have already been soaked off.

Packets, quantities of stamps by country or by theme, are generally off paper. For example, thumbing through one dealer's price list at random, you may see that you can pay $49.50 for 2,000 stamps from Africa; $1.65 for 25 stamps from Barbados; $6.30 for 500 stamps from Czechoslovakia (or, if you want all of the stamps to be pictorials, $8.25); $6.20 for 400 stamps depicting animals; $4.40 for 100 Disney stamps; $6.50 for 100 stamps hon-

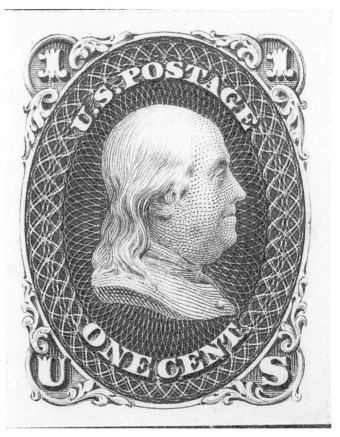

Two early one-cent stamps. The one on the left was issued in 1851, the one on the right in 1861. During that ten year period, the U.S. began perforating its stamps, which made it easier to separate them. Imperforate stamps had to be cut apart with scissors, and unless the user had a very steady hand, uneven cuts were the rule—note especially the bottom of the stamp on the left, which was cut at an angle.

oring John F. Kennedy; or $30.50 for 350 stamps with other designs on them.

Be sure to buy packets that are sold as *all different*, as opposed to *assorted*. "100 assorted" just means that you will get 100 stamps—and that may include duplication. If the packet says "100 all different," you'll get 100 different stamps.

It's also important to understand that if you buy a packet that's touted as, "1,000 stamps total catalog value $50 for only $5," for example, don't buy it thinking you're going to become a multimillionaire. An assemblage of one thousand stamps totaling $50 in value means that each stamp is worth a nickel. The dealer preparing an assortment like this can afford to do so because stamps worth 5¢ are available in quantity from wholesalers at even

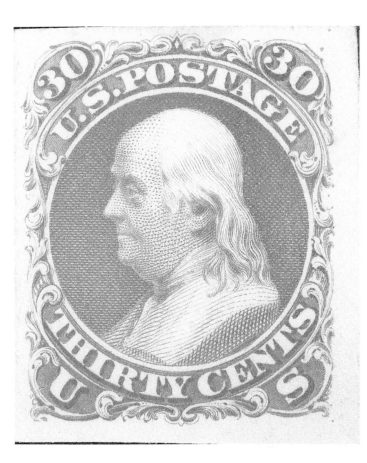

This 1861 thirty-cent stamp depicts Benjamin Franklin. Franklin, and George Washington, were among the most frequent subjects of early U.S. stamps.

lower prices. So while it's true that those 1,000 stamps combined have a catalog value of $50, *you* won't be able to get that kind of money for them. Besides, when stamps catalog as low as 5¢ per stamp, their true value is really negligible, and the 5¢ figure actually represents more the dealer's time and expense in being able to offer that stamp for sale than any actual value. (This is not to say that a 5¢ stamp is useless. After all, no collection can be truly complete without such a stamp.)

Approvals

Approvals are another good way to buy stamps; and you get to see the stamps before you buy them. On request, an approval dealer will send you a selection of stamps for your inspection. You return the stamps you don't want and keep the ones you do (and pay for them, of course). However, if any stamps are lost or damaged while you have them, you have to pay for them. Approval dealers generally allow you ten days to look over the stamps.

Don't confuse approvals with *want lists*, where you send a dealer a list of stamps you're interested in. The dealer will go over your list, review the stock, and let you know what is available at what price. You're under no obligation to buy, but it is courteous to write back to let the dealer know whether or not you want the stamps so that they can be sold to another customer.

Auctions

Another way collectors buy stamps is by *auction*. You can attend an auction in person or bid through the mail. In fact, some auctions are by mail only. Auctions are serious business; when participating in an auction by mail, it's very important to know the terms of sale of the auction. Terms are listed in the auction catalog, and when you send in your bids you will have to sign a statement saying that you agree to abide by them. If there's a dispute, and you claim you didn't know the rules, that won't count for anything, even if you really *didn't* know.

You are also responsible for making sure your bids are accurate. Suppose you want lot 94 and are willing to bid $50 for it. But, if for some reason or another—maybe you get distracted while filling out the bid sheet—you wind up writing 93 instead of 94, the auction house will execute your request as a bid of $50 for lot 93. If you win lot 93, you're stuck with it, and someone else will get lot 94—which can be quite painful if, based on your intended bid, you would have won lot 94. And, to add insult to injury, suppose lot 93, which you just paid $50 for, is worth only $10. That's why it's very important to be extremely careful when you place a bid by mail.

But on the good side of auctions, some houses sell lots at set increments over the second-highest bids. Let's say

1879: First postage-due stamps are issued. They were discontinued in 1985.

A postage-due stamp from 1930. Postage-due stamps were issued in the U.S. from 1879 to 1985, when their use was discontinued (although they still collect for postage due—they just don't issue special stamps for that purpose anymore).

you want lot 100 (yes, this time you *do* write 100 on your bid sheet), and for this lot you're also going to place a bid of $50. Yours is the top bid, and you win the lot. However, this auction house sells its lots at a certain amount over the second-highest bid, as printed in the catalog. In this case, the second-highest bid for lot 100 was $30. So, you would have to pay only $33 ($30 plus $3, which is one step up)—$17 less than what you were willing to pay. Of course, you should always be prepared to pay the amount you are willing to bid; it's stupid to bid $1,000 when you can only afford $50, hoping the second-highest bid is $35. And if someone else wants the lot just as badly as you do and bids $900, you're in the hole for one step above, or $990.

Stamp auctions are taken very seriously. If you attend one in person, you'll find that it's quite easy to get caught

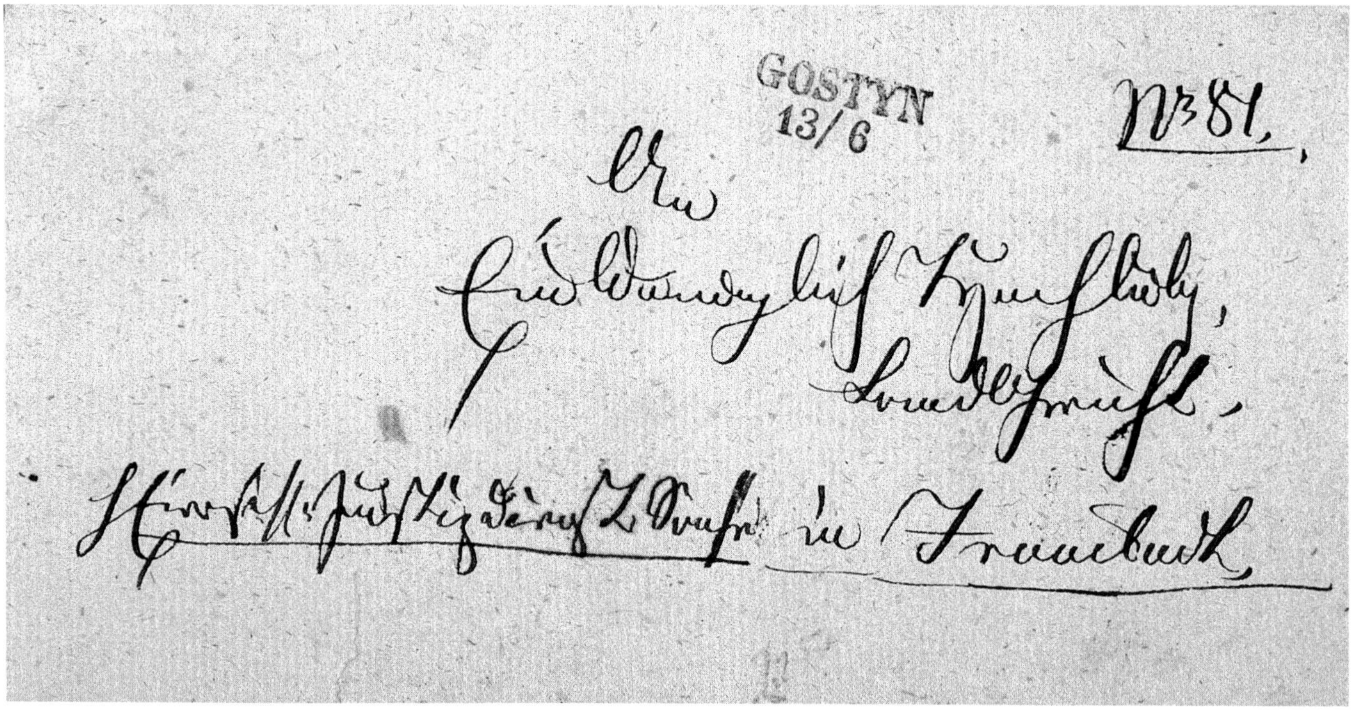
GOSTYN
13/6
Nº 81

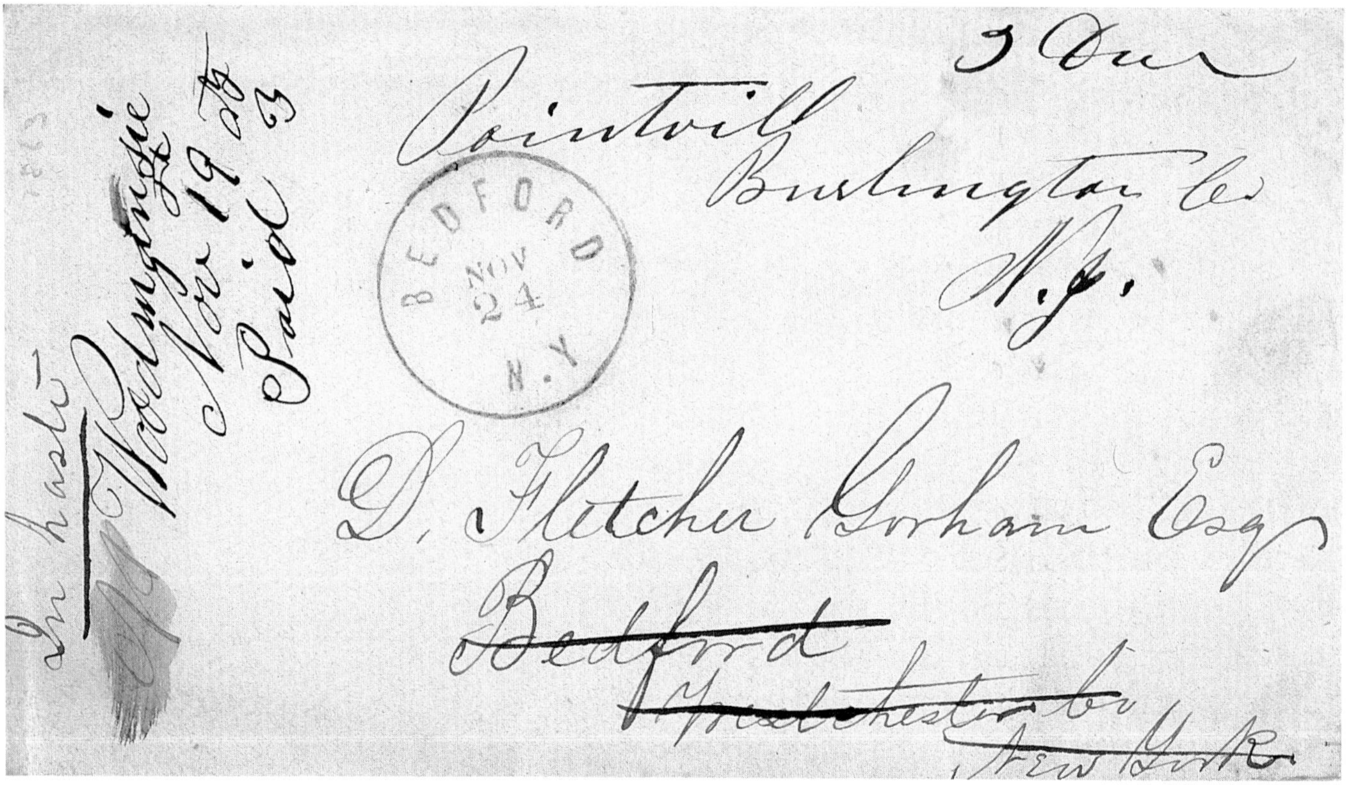
BEDFORD
NOV
24
N.Y
D. Fletcher Gorham Esq
Bedford
Burlington Co
N.J.
New York
Nov 19
Paid 3

up in the frenzy of bidding and winning. If you want certain extremely rare stamps, auctions are the only way you'll be able to try to buy them.

Money for Nothing

Stamps are receipts that entitle you to postal services equivalent to their face value. Each stamp that is saved and not used represents pure profit for the post office. This presents plenty of incentive for postal administrations to issue stamps that would be of extra interest to collectors.

Don't think that postal administrations are unaware of this. It costs very little money to print a stamp. There are many countries that grind out lots of new stamps a year. They're colorful; they're attractive; and they usually commemorate subjects that are popular with stamp collectors. The only problem is that these kinds of stamps see very little use in their own country. Many collectors derisively refer to such stamps as wallpaper.

One way to tell if stamps are closer to being wallpaper than legitimate postal stamps is to see if they feature subjects that are seemingly of little interest to their own citizens. Would you be interested in an American stamp that commemorates a British soccer club? Oddly the island of St. Vincent, in the West Indies, has issued stamps commemorating the 1988 World Series and the 1989 Los Angeles Dodgers Team. St. Vincent has issued many stamps depicting American baseball players of the past and present—baseball cards and baseball memorabilia are very collectible these days, and the presumption is that along with philatelists, sports collectors will want these stamps. These stamps have in fact been advertised in baseball-card publications as well.

Some collectors look upon these kinds of stamps with contempt, because they see them as nothing more than glorified labels. It's not the subject matter per se that offends them—the United States has issued stamps hon-

A stampless cover from the eighteenth century (opposite, top). It has a handstamped "13/6" (thirteen shillings, sixpence) rate marking. A stampless cover from Bedford, New York (opposite, bottom). The original address was invalid, so a forwarding address was written in and three cents postage due was assessed (said deficiency noted in manuscript). Covers such as these are very collectible because they show particular rates, services, etc.

1886: The American Philatelic Society, the country's largest philatelic organization, is founded.

oring Jackie Robinson (1982), Babe Ruth (1983), Roberto Clemente (1984), and Lou Gehrig (1989), as well as stamps honoring the sport of baseball itself (1939 and 1969). Many collectors save the United States baseball stamps, but many more people use these stamps on their mail, so that's okay. It's the issues from faraway places, where the natives have never heard of most of today's players, that collectors look on with suspicion.

Other kinds of stamps in strange formats have been self-adhesive, cut-to-shape from Tonga and Sierra Leone; three-dimensional; plastic-embossed; and even a miniature record that actually plays, all from Bhutan.

The United States has also issued its share of stamps in unusual formats, but the philatelic community accepts them because they know that they *can* be used for postage. These stamps have been discussed in the Introduction: self-adhesives (1974 and 1989), a prestamped envelope with a hologram in the design (1989), and even *plastic* stamps, designed to be sold through bank ATM machines (1990).

The author of this book holds to the belief that people should collect whatever they like. Your collection has no bearing on anyone else's—and no other collection has any bearing on yours. But you should be aware that many collectors look down on these stamps and dismiss them as nothing more than money-making gimmicks designed to sucker the gullible. If you buy such stamps with the attitude of "I *know* it's a money-making gimmick designed to sucker the gullible, but I don't care; I like it and I *still* want it," that's about all anyone can ask of you.

1893: The United States' first series of commemorative stamps, honoring the World Columbian Exposition and the four-hundredth anniversary of the discovery of America, are issued.

Two stamps from the 1893 World's Columbian Exposition.

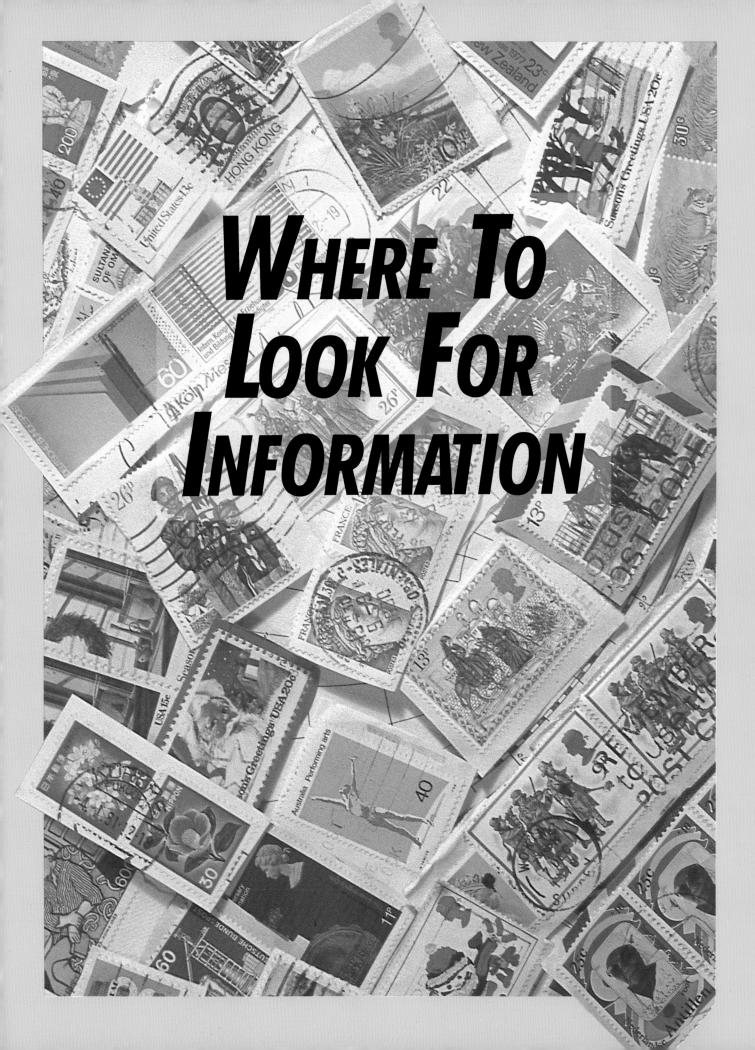

WHERE TO LOOK FOR INFORMATION

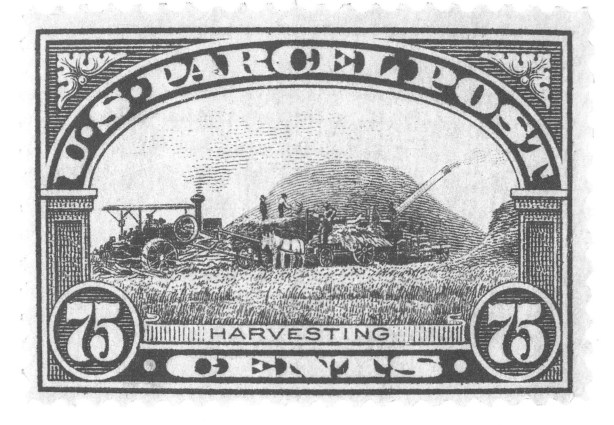

This seventy-five-cent parcel post stamp was issued in 1913. Philately is blessed with specialized works explaining various aspects of stamp collecting and postal history, such as the parcel post, in far greater scope than a basic book such as this can. To a beginner, some of the more detailed works might seem especially arcane—but should you ever develop a specific interest and want to learn more about it, you'll be grateful the books are available.

A guaranteed method of learning about stamps is reading about them as much as possible. This should be an enjoyable and even entertaining endeavor. Whether you see reading about stamps as pleasure or work, the fact is that the more you know about stamps, the more enjoyment you'll derive from your collection. On some rainy afternoon, you might want to wile away the hours perusing one of these luxurious volumes: *The Modern Prestamped Envelopes of Australia; Censorship of the Civil Mails in Occupied Austria, 1945–1953; Cancellations of the Treaty Ports of Hong Kong, 1850–1930; Confederate States of America: Markings and Postal History of Richmond, Virginia.*

On second thought, maybe not—at least not right now.

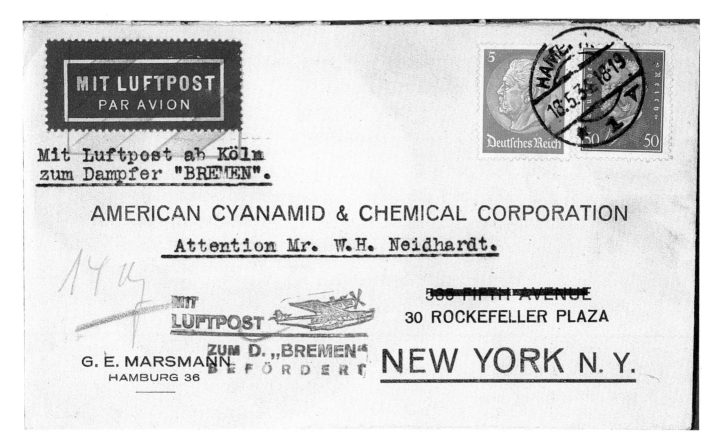

It's quite understandable, actually, that some of you out there are reading these titles and thinking, "What kinds of people *write* books like these?" They don't get out much, do they? Well, books such as these might seem obscure and baffling to the beginner, but to the specialist whose interests lie in these fields, these are very welcome sources of information, which will help enhance their own collections. Who knows, maybe *you'll* write a specialized book one day! But right now, you'll probably be better off reading something general.

A ship-to-shore catapult cover used on letters that were ''shot'' to shore from ships. Many philatelists are interested in the various methods postal people have used to move the mail, and covers such as these are collectible because of how they were transmitted. Again, philatelic literature is the key to unlocking all of the mysteries of stamp collecting and postal services.

BASIC READING

The Postal Service Guide to U.S. Stamps has already been discussed in the previous chapter. It's a good first refer-

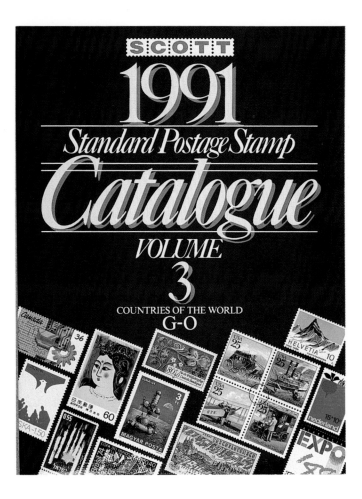

Cover of the Scott Catalogue, 1991 edition. The major stamp catalogue used in the U.S., Scott covers the world of stamps in five volumes. Shown is the cover to Volume 3, over 1,100 pages listing the stamps issued from countries G to O (Gabon to Oltre Giuba).

ence work for you to have, but by no means is it *the* definitive catalog of American stamps, nor is it the *official* catalog, even though it is published by the Postal Service.

The most widely used catalog in the United States is the *Scott Catalogue,* named after pioneering stamp and coin dealer J. Walter Scott, who founded the catalog in the 1860s as his retail price list. The numbering system used in the *Scott Catalogue* has become the standard method in the United States for identifying a particular stamp. If you want, for example, the 13¢ commemorative from 1976 that publicized the international stamp show Interphil '76, you'd simply ask for Sc. 1632. (Scott is usually abbreviated *Sc.*) The aforementioned *Postal Service Guide to U.S. Stamps* uses *Scott Catalogue* numbers—and, when a new stamp is announced, the Postal Service press release also includes the *Scott* number for the new stamp.

Today, the *Scott Catalogue* is published in five volumes:
• *Volume 1* covers the United States plus the British Commonwealth of Nations;
• *Volume 2* covers all other countries from A to F;
• *Volume 3* covers countries from G to O;
• *Volume 4* covers the rest of the world from P to Z;
• The fifth volume is a specialized catalog of United States stamps that lists issues in greater detail than *Volume 1* and also has listings for local stamps, revenues, plate blocks, and more. It even lists Christmas seals!

Unfortunately, the catalogs are not cheap. Each volume has a suggested list price of $26; the set of five costs $130. However, most public libraries do have a set or two of the *Scott* catalog, even if not the most recent edition, so you can certainly go there and browse through a volume or even borrow one.

Two of America's major stamp weeklies—Stamp Collector and Linn's Stamp News. Linn's is owned by Amos Press of Sidney, Ohio, the same company that publishes the Scott Catalogue, and is the largest philatelic newspaper in the country. Both newspapers are worth reading, and you should subscribe to at least one of them.

CERTIFIED MAIL

U.S. POSTAGE 15¢

This certified mail stamp, showing a smiling letter carrier, was issued in 1955 and was the only stamp ever issued for this purpose. The Scott Catalogue identifies this stamp as Sc. FA1. Other catalogues use different numbering systems to identify their stamps—Britain's Stanley Gibbons catalogue, for example, lists it as C1070. Numbering systems are not interchangeable—if you want to buy this stamp, ask for FA1, not C1070 (Scott uses the ''C'' prefix for airmail stamps, and based on Scott's numbering the U.S. hasn't issued stamp C200 yet, let alone C1000!).

Other countries have their own dominant specialist catalog publishers and their own catalog numbering systems. The United Kingdom, for example, has the *Stanley Gibbons* catalog (also named after an old-time dealer), and its numbering system differs from *Scott*'s.

Scott separates stamps intended for specific purposes (airmail, special delivery, and so on) from commemorative and regular postage, while *Gibbons* basically integrates everything into one listing. For example, the United States' one-and-only stamp issued for certified mail (a 15¢ stamp from 1955 that shows a letter carrier) is listed in *Scott* as FA1 (FA being the prefix for certified-mail

If your interests go beyond the stamps and into the operations of the Postal Service itself, the *Domestic Mail Manual* will serve your needs. It's the official book of postal laws and regulations. There are a few sections dealing with philately, in terms of what the Postal Service can do to accommodate stamp collectors, but it's mostly the nuts-and-bolts rule book for the folks behind the counter.

The *Domestic Mail Manual* is available to the general public on a subscription basis (it's updated four times a year), so you might want to take out a subscription. For more information, write to the Superintendent of Documents, Government Printing Office, Washington, DC 20402-9371.

Another official postal publication you might be interested in is the Postal Bulletin, shown below. It comes out regularly and includes changes in Domestic Mail Manual regulations, announcements of new stamps, and the like. It's available to the public on a subscription basis from the Superintendent of Documents, same address as shown in the box to your left. But keep in mind that this is very much an in-house publication, designed expressly for postal employees; it includes pages that are intended to be torn out and posted on post office walls, such as post office holidays, safety messages, etc. One issue consisted primarily of a list of names and addresses of health care providers that postal workers could choose from. The Postal Bulletin is not designed for philatelists, but if your postal interests are that strong you might find it interesting.

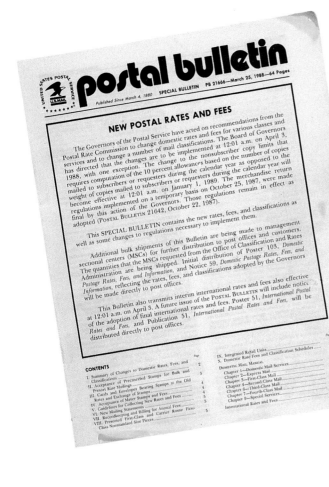
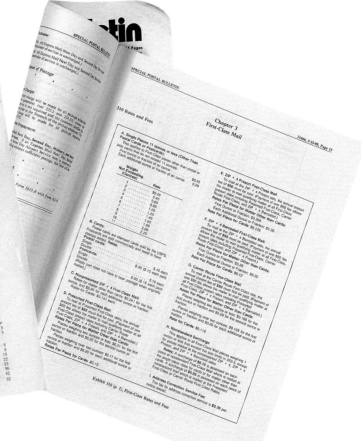

stamps), while British collectors know it as C1070; it falls between regular numbers 1069 and 1070. (That is, *Gibbons* simply assigns it the same number as the next sequential regular issue or commemorative, but adds a letter prefix based on what kind of stamp it is. A *C* in front of a *Scott* catalog number, on the other hand, indicates an airmail stamp. The famous 24¢ stamp with the upside-down plane is *Scott* catalog number C3a, because it's an airmail stamp.) Other countries' dominant catalogs are *Yvert and Ceres* (France), *Michel* (Germany), *Facit* (Scandinavia) and *Zumstein* (Switzerland).

Another reference work you might want to have is the *Linn's World Stamp Almanac,* almost one thousand pages of information on all sorts of matters relating to postal service in the United States. For example, it includes the history of the posts, postal rates, postmasters general, postal regulations, philately and the law, stamp organizations, major stamp auctions, famous stamp collectors, and yes, philatelic literature.

Philatelic literature is wonderful reading. Some editions of selected works of literature are collectible themselves, but the information you can get out of them is absolutely priceless.

I Read the News Today, Oh Boy...

In addition to reference books and annual catalogs, Philately also has its own weekly newspapers. It's recommended that you subscribe to at least one of them. Sample a few issues of each, so you can get a feel for what interests you. What the author likes doesn't mean a thing to you. Your personal taste should guide the overall course of your collection.

The three major stamp weeklies are:

Linn's Stamp News, P.O. Box 29, Sidney, OH 45365-0029

Stamp Collector, Box 10, Albany, OR 97321-0006

Stamps, 85 Canisteo Street, Hornell, NY 14843-1544.

If you join a national stamp society (listed in Appendix), you'll receive its publication. Society journals are very interesting, and many intriguing articles appear in these publications, often the result of many years of research.

One disadvantage is that the journals are not necessarily geared toward the newcomer, and you might feel daunted when you read one for the first time. But don't let that stop you—just jump right in and do the best you can. Before you know it, you'll find that you'll understand exactly what's going on. As time goes by, when you reread your first issues of the society journals, you'll fondly remember your philatelic innocence. You might even find *yourself* contributing to your favorite journal someday. Editors are always on the lookout for material to publish, so don't feel intimidated. Think of it this way: Every expert started out as a beginner.

SPECIALIZATION

The three-cent issue from the 1893 World's Columbian Exposition issue.

The first stamp was issued in Great Britain in 1840. In the 150 years that have since passed, lots of stamps have been issued. The United States alone has issued more than twenty-five hundred stamps—and Russia has issued more than six thousand! Add the stamps issued by all of the other countries, and you can come to the conclusion that it would be just about impossible to collect one example of each stamp ever issued. There are some stamps of which only *one* specimen is known to exist. This means that, at any given moment it is possible for *only one person* in the world to have a truly complete collection of every stamp ever issued.

So, what's the next step? Why bother even beginning, if you can't ever have a totally complete collection? This is the reason for specialization.

Specialization. It is an intimidating word. You see in your mind's eye a group of elderly collectors analyzing an old stamp to death, viewing it through a 100,000-enlargement-power microscope, searching for that line 1/100 of a millimeter long that shows it to be a rare variety that was issued on every stamp in position 58 on sheets printed on plate A11365–2925.

The four-cent issue from the 1893 World's Columbian Exposition issue. This stamp and the one shown on the opposite page both depict ships and would qualify for inclusion in a topical collection based on ships or sailing.

SELECTING A CATEGORY

Actually, specialization can be a lot of fun. Specialization just means picking one aspect of philately and concentrating on that. Specialization is a broad term. It *could* mean scrutinizing one stamp for minute details—but it could also mean collecting stamps that relate to your country,

1918: Airmail service begins. The first cities to receive airmail service are New York and Washington, D.C.

your job, your religion, or whatever interests you have. It can be *anything* you like.

And that's an important factor. Whatever you do decide to collect, make sure that you're collecting something *you* like. Your stamp collection is there for you to enjoy, and you'll be spending your time and money on it, so don't worry if someone else doesn't like what you've chosen to collect.

One form of specialization is known as *topical* collecting, in which you collect according to the topic the stamps commemorate, regardless of which country issued them. Topical collecting can also involve objects on stamps. For instance, the 1990 United States commemorative honor-

These three stamps comprise the 1930 Graf Zeppelin issue, issued for use on letters carried aboard the Graf Zeppelin. These stamps were sold for a short period of time, and today they're among the most prized of all U.S. stamps.

ing the poet Marianne Moore would be of interest to those who collect women on stamps, writers on stamps, or even famous people who died in the 1970s.

There really are no rules in specialization, because you decide how far you want to go. But you should use some common sense when you define the parameters you use to select your specialization. On the one hand, you can define your specialty as "whatever appeals to me at the moment I'm buying my stamps"; or your goals can be as narrow as "used examples of the 1962 United States Sam Rayburn commemorative, canceled with a Brooklyn, New York, postmark dated September 20, 1962."

Choosing the latter will undoubtedly make for a frus-

Christmas USA 1981

Botticelli: Art Institute of Chicago

1981 religious U.S. Christmas issue (left), and a 1975 U.S. secular Christmas issue (opposite). The U.S. issues two Christmas stamps each year, one religious and one non-religious. Adding to the significance of the stamps on this spread is the fact that neither one bears a printed face value, since they were issued at times when postal rates were scheduled to increase and the value of these stamps could not be definitely set until after they were printed. The 1975 stamp, face value ten cents, was one of the first nondenominated stamps ever issued by the United States. (The 1981 stamp is worth twenty cents.)

Themes for topical collections

Advertising	Christmas	Gandhi	Living People on	Public	Stadiums and
Animals	Winston Churchill	Sir Rowland Hill	Stamps	Transportation	Arenas
Antarctica	Cinema	(the inventor	Maps	Rock Stars	Stamps on
Anti-malaria	Concorde	of postage	Marine Life	Franklin D.	Stamps
Art	Captain Cook	stamps)	Medicine	Roosevelt	Submarines
Automobiles	Copernicus	Horses	Music	Royalty	Trains
Aviation	Costumes	Insects	New York City	Scientists	United Nations
Baseball	Charles de Gaulle	John F. Kennedy	Nuclear Energy	Scouting	Universal Postal
Birds	Dogs	Judaica	Nudes	Seashells	Union
Bridges	Europe	Martin Luther	Olympics	Ships	Whales
Butterflies	Fish	King	Orchids	Soccer	Women
Cats	Flags	Abraham Lincoln	Paintings	Space	World's Fair
Chess	Flowers	Lions Club	Petroleum	Sports	Zeppelins

trating search (how many of those can there be, anyway?), so keep in mind that the broader you make your specialty, the easier it will be to find material to add to your collection.

SUPPLIES

It's not enough just to buy stamps, or even to buy stamps and literature. You also need a place to put your stamps. You can't just throw them all in a shoebox and forget about them. You need a special implement for handling stamps, as well as a perforation gauge and a watermark detector. Is this starting to sound like one of those *Enjoying Your Turtle*-type of books? You probably thought all you had to do to be a stamp collector was get some stamps and put them in a safe place, but you're finding out that you also need to buy this and you have to do that and you must know about this other thing over here. But at least you don't have to feed stamps, and stamps don't die. All of this effort *is* worth it—you'll see.

Shown on these two pages are different kinds of printed stamp albums. The one on the left has what is known as post binding, which can be expanded to add more pages —either blank pages to store stamps the printed pages don't cover, or printed supplements covering stamps issued after the bulk of the album was printed. A spiral-bound album is on the right—this kind doesn't allow for more pages, but tends to be less expensive.

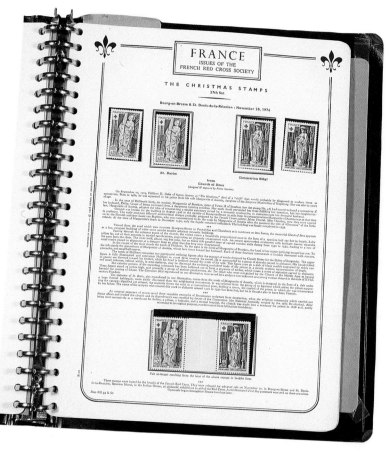

WHERE TO STORE YOUR STAMPS

You don't need to set up a whole room in your house as a miniature archival storage center for your stamps. The day may come when you find you need something like that, but that's not your immediate concern.

Many collectors put their stamps in *albums.* Stamp albums have nothing to do with vinyl LPs. Rather, in their most basic form, stamp albums are binders with pages that are specially designed for storing stamps.

There are two general kinds of albums—*printed* and *blank.* Printed albums have pictures of every stamp, and

This is a blank album page, with handwritten notations. It differs from a printed page in that the collector was able to design it based on his personal tastes, creating a sense of individuality you just can't get from a mass-produced printed page. The collector also added his own notes about each stamp. If you feel printed albums are a little on the restrictive side, you might want to use blank album pages—where you're the one who decides how each page should appear. A blank page is a must if you decide to assemble a collection based on topics or themes for which there are no printed pages available.

you're supposed to place the stamp over that picture. If you plan to collect conventionally—that is, acquire one example of each stamp issued by a given country and mount them in catalog order—a printed album might be best, especially for newcomers, since all you have to do is look for the picture of the stamp you have and mount the stamp over it. *Don't lick the stamp and then stick it in.* If you do, you're reducing the stamp's value to that of waste paper. Later on, we'll discuss how to put stamps in albums (or mount them, to use the correct term).

Blank albums don't specify which stamps should go where, which is an advantage if you want to determine your own layout. For example, the *Scott* catalog does *not* necessarily present its stamps in chronological order, and if you decide to store your stamps in the order in which

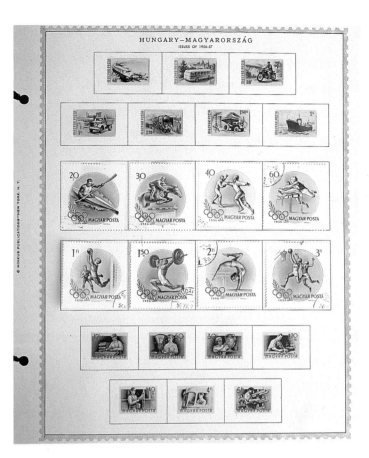

A two-ring album similar to the traditional three-ring school binders. You can add new pages just as easily to this kind of page as you can with a post-binding album.

they were issued, a printed album is not for you. Printed albums are generally sold by country, but some manufacturers make pages designed for topical collecting. With such albums you'd be assembling your collection based on what the *manufacturer* decided should be included in a given topic—whereas you might decide, based on your interests, that a given stamp doesn't fit into your definition of a particular topic.

Regardless of whether you buy a printed album or a blank one, you're much better off buying one that's printed only on one side. Albums printed on both sides of the pages entail a risk of stamps on facing pages coming into contact, and if that happens there's a chance that stamps might grab and pull at one another. However, albums with pages printed on both sides are more eco-

1920: Postage meters are introduced.

1921: The United States inaugurates the world's first philatelic agency, a branch of the post office devoted especially to serving the needs of stamp collectors. Today, many large cities have philatelic windows. They serve the same basic function as the philatelic agency, which still exists today in the form of the Philatelic Sales Division.

nomical, so one alternative is using some kind of interweaving between the pages, which will prevent stamps on facing pages from touching one another.

Another kind of book you can use is a *stock book,* which is a blank book with pockets for you to insert stamps. The biggest advantage of stock books is that stamps can be easily inserted and removed, without the use of hinges or mounts. Stock books are not printed, though, and they're used primarily by dealers as one method of storing their stock (hence the name). Even if you decide to store your stamps in an album, an inexpensive stock book might be a good place for you to keep duplicate or unsorted stamps.

PLACING YOUR STAMPS IN ALBUMS

There are two ways to place stamps in albums. The more traditional method is by the use of a *stamp hinge.* A hinge is a small, folded piece of paper that is gummed on one side. You moisten the tip of the smaller end (leave the area near the fold dry so you'll able to lift the stamp when it's in the album). Then place the hinge on the back of the stamp, near the top (but just below the perforations, so when you're looking at the stamp you don't actually see the hinge), then moisten the larger end and affix that to the album page. Hinges are removable, so you don't have to worry if you stick it in the wrong place (either on the stamp or in your album), but you do have to wait until the hinge has dried before you remove it, otherwise you could damage the stamp.

The disadvantage to hinges is that they remove some of the gum, and many stamps are worth more (*lots* more) with full gum. (You can hinge a used stamp with impunity, because the gum will have been removed when the stamp was soaked off the envelope.)

The most popular alternative to hinges are *stamp mounts,* which are basically clear plastic sleeves that

A stock book (below) is a very easy place to store your stamps. It has page-wide pockets in which to insert your stamps, and there is no printing, so you can keep stamps in any order until you're ready to put them in your album—unless you want to use a stock book as an album, which is perfectly fine. This souvenir sheet (right) was issued in 1934 for the National Stamp Exhibition in New York City. It consists of six examples of stamps issued four months earlier honoring the Byrd Antarctic Expedition of 1933.

The proper way to handle stamps is with stamp tongs—not tweezers, but stamp tongs. You might damage a stamp if you held it in your hand—and this particular stamp, the famous inverted Jenny (simply the most expensive of all United States stamps, selling for six figures) is one stamp you most definitely do not want to damage.

are gummed on the back. Since the gummed part of the mount doesn't touch the stamp, the gum on the stamp is safe.

STAMP TONGS

Stamps should be handled as infrequently as possible. In their most basic description, stamps are gummed bits of paper—quite fragile ones, at that—and even if you just handle a stamp regularly you might bend it, get it dirty, or otherwise damage it. Collectors use *tongs*, which are like tweezers, except that the inside edges of tongs (the edges that actually touch the stamp) are flat. Never use ordinary tweezers in lieu of tongs.

Tongs come in all different sizes and point tips, but for

beginners, the best kind to buy is a pair with wide tips. As you advance, you may find it advantageous to buy narrow-pointed tongs, which allow maximum visibility of the stamp.

PERFORATION GAUGES

In the Beatles song "A Day In the Life," there's a line about four thousand holes in Blackburn, Lancashire, and the singer having to count them all. Counting holes sounds ludicrous, but in philately it's vital. The holes we're talking about make up the perforations, and in some stamps a difference in perforations can make the difference between a cheap stamp and a very expensive one.

A stamp's perforations are determined by the number of holes there are in 2 centimeters (.75 inch). A stamp identified as perf 12 means that it has twelve perforation holes in each 2-centimeter increment. Some stamps have different perforations along the top and the sides. Such perforations are called compound perfs, and the perforations along the top line are given first. A stamp identified as perf 11 × 10 means that the top and bottom of the stamp have 11 perforations for every 2 centimeters, and the left and right sides have 10 for every 2 centimeters.

How can you tell how many perforations a stamp has? One method is to use a ruler that measures in centimeters, and then count each hole until you reach the 2-centimeter mark. It's wiser and more efficient, however, to obtain a *perforation gauge*, which is essentially a ruler made for measuring stamp perforations. A perforation gauge can be made of cardboard, metal, or plastic, and it's absolutely essential.

WATERMARKS

A *watermark* is a design that appears as a thin spot on a stamp when you hold it up to the light. Watermarks serve as a security measure to prevent counterfeiting. Like perforations, watermarks can have a major effect on a

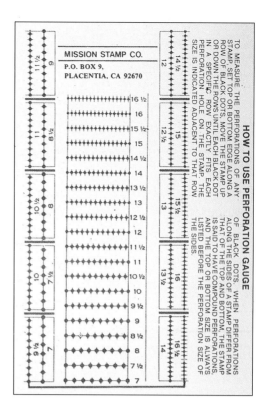

A typical perforation gauge. In some cases, the perforations are the sole distinction between a cheap stamp and an expensive one, and this little device can tell you which version you have. This particular gauge also includes directions on how to use it.

Another form of collecting is saving stamps with marginal inscriptions (opposite, top)—printing (plate numbers or any other kind of markings) in the selvage. Shown is a 1901 one-cent Pan American Exposition commemorative strip of three, with a plate number and a printer's imprint in the selvage. This U.S. commemorative honoring the centennial of Wyoming's statehood (opposite, bottom) was issued in 1990. Postal policy at the time the stamp came out was to not put the year of issue on the stamp, hence the lone date "1890." This policy is not popular with many collectors, and it has been reported that some thought the stamp was issued in 1890. Also note the expression of the denomination as "25" instead of "25¢"—standard practice since late 1984.

stamp's value, so it's good to have some watermark fluid and a watermark tray.

Watermark fluid is a special kind of liquid that you can safely put on the back of a stamp without affecting the gum. A watermark tray is a dark plastic tray that helps the watermark stand out more clearly, when watermark fluid is put on the back of the stamp.

You should be very careful with watermark fluid, because some kinds are flammable. Other kinds are toxic if you breathe too much of the fumes, so always make sure there's plenty of ventilation where you're using watermark fluid. Also, be aware that some fluids can melt plastic stamp mounts.

MAGNIFYING GLASSES

A stereotypical image of a stamp collector, as alluded to in the previous chapter, is that of an old man hunched over a microscope, intensely scrutinizing a stamp, searching for some obscure marking.

On some of the very early stamps, it may be some obscure marking that makes the difference between a cheap stamp and a very valuable one. A magnifying glass is another vital tool for the philatelist. It can help you easily see the intricacies of engraved designs and notice "secret marks" that some engravers unobtrusively put in some stamp designs.

At the beginning stage, you don't need anything fancy. Any regular magnifying glass you already have will do. Of course, for more expensive stamps where miniscule differences do influence the value, you might need a more powerful magnifying glass.

DEALING WITH DEALERS

Left: The 1863 ''Black Jack'' two-cent stamp, so-called because of its color (black) and subject (Andrew Jackson), is popular among advanced collectors because of the various fancy cancellations that appear on it. The presence of certain cancellations can greatly affect the value of this stamp. Well-centered specimens are more valuable— back in those days, the printers were mainly concerned with printing the stamps and getting them to the post office. Centering was not a priority.

For you, the collector, stamp collecting is a hobby, a way to spend some hard-earned leisure time. And when you want to add some material to your collection, you go to a stamp store. Just imagine a place where all they do is eat, drink, and sleep stamps.

You know that the grass is always greener on the other side, right? One important thing you have to realize is that while dealers may be working in an environment they enjoy and get pleasure out of, stamps are more than a hobby.

Stamps are the dealer's livelihood. It's not easy to run a business these days, and just like any other retailer, the dealer has expenses to meet: rent, salaries, utilities, advertising, membership in professional trade organizations, and more. The only difference is that, unlike the

First Day Cover
RE-VALUED
ENVELOPE
Feb. 5, 1968
Washington, D. C.

WASHINGTON
FEB 5
AM
1968
D. C.

U.S. POSTAGE
5¢

First Day Covers are a very popular collecting specialty—envelopes postmarked with the first day a new postal item is issued. This is a First Day Cover of a revalued six-cent prestamped envelope (the government took unsold five-cent envelopes, imprinted a one-cent ''stamp'' to the left of the design, and sold them for six cents). The inscription in the upper left corner was privately printed.

guy who runs the grocery store, the stamp dealer is not selling something you need to survive.

Unfortunately, the local stamp store is not as common a sight as it used to be. They're still around, though, especially in larger cities, so don't get discouraged.

1937: A special "First Day of Issue" cancellation is put into use. Before this, regular postmarks were used on First Day Covers.

VISITING THE STAMP STORE

If you do have access to a stamp store, you'll find that the dealer can be very valuable to you, especially while you're a beginner. Dealers work with stamps all day, so they can give you the best advice on caring for your collection, what to buy and what not to buy, and so on in a personal manner that this book cannot.

A booklet pane of six one-cent stamps from the long-running ''Presidentials'' definitive series (1938-1954). Each stamp depicted a deceased president, from George Washington (one-cent) to Calvin Coolidge ($5). Benjamin Franklin, Martha Washington, and the White House are also included in the series.

This is not always a given, however, because of many circumstances. Maybe a particular dealer is not receptive to being your mentor, if you will, either because of his or her nature, or because there isn't enough time to work with and help educate beginning collectors. (Such an attitude is unfortunate, because it's in a dealer's best interest to cultivate as many new collectors as possible. New collectors mean new customers, and new customers mean more potential repeat business.)

Being a stamp dealer's acquaintance can be a valuable asset. Let's say, for example, you have a special interest in stamps from a particular country, but your dealer doesn't routinely sell that kind of material. Your dealer probably knows someone who does, and can refer you there or obtain the item for you. The majority of dealers are fair and ethical, and they want you to keep coming back to their store to buy more stamps.

ORDERING BY MAIL

Those who don't have easy access to a stamp store (*and* those who do) can buy stamps by *mail order.* If you're into instant gratification, this is a most frustrating way to buy, because you're not getting your stamps immediately. But then again, you'll be able to look forward to receiving something nice in the mail (the stamps you ordered), so that makes up for it.

One benefit of mail order is that it gives you a greater opportunity to compare prices. A reality of working with stamp dealers in person, especially if you continually pick their brains for advice, is that in return they do expect you to do at least some of your stamp buying from them. (It's not fair to constantly go to dealer A for advice, only to spend your money at dealer B's store—even if B's prices *are* lower than A's.)

When dealing with a mail-order stamp dealer for the first time, it's best to make a small order instead of a large one. By doing so, you will be able to see what kind of serv-

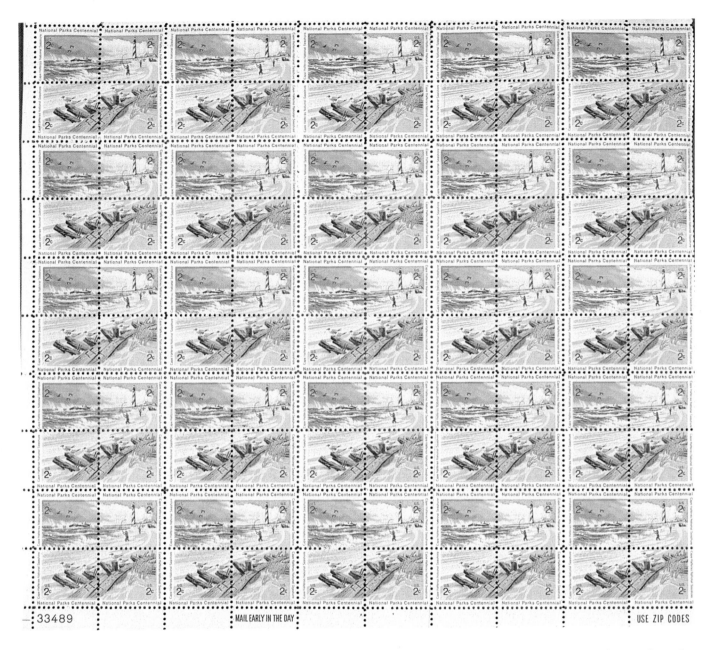

One of the more interesting United States stamps, this is a full sheet of the 1972 Cape Hatteras National Seashore block of four. Four stamps are necessary to make up the complete design.

Ironically, each of these stamps has a face value of two cents, and the First Class letter rate in 1972 was eight cents—meaning a whole block of four was needed to mail a letter.

This block of four, issued in 1969 for the Eleventh International Botanical Congress in Seattle, is known as a "se-tenant" issue because all four designs are joined together at the perforation. Each stamp in a se-tenant issue can be an independent design, such as these, or make up a larger design over a number of stamps (as with the Hatteras stamps shown on page 83).

ice the dealer provides. Also, on the off chance that the dealer is a rip-off artist, your losses will not be too great.

When you order by mail, make sure your name and address are on the letter itself, not just on the outside envelope. Some dealers separate the envelope from the rest of the order (they can always sell the used stamps they get from their incoming mail—that's one way packets and mixtures are assembled), and if your name and address are not on the letter, the dealer isn't going to know where to send the stamps.

You should also keep a record of your purchases—preferably a photocopy of your letter and a photocopy of your check or money order. If there's a dispute, having proof of payment will go a very long way toward resolving the problem in your favor.

STAMP SHOWS

Stamp shows are a good way to immerse yourself in the world of stamps. A stamp show (sometimes called a Pex, for *P*hilatelic *Ex*hibition) is essentially a flea market or minimall with nothing but stamps on exhibit. Stamp shows usually take place over two to three days, including a weekend. They're usually run by local stamp clubs, although the ASDA also sponsors its own shows. There is usually an admission charge to get in.

The exhibits are a good way for you to look at material you probably would not see otherwise or be able to afford. Most exhibits are competitive in nature; that is, they are competing for prizes and awards.

But the most interesting and useful stamp shows also have a *bourse,* where dealers have their booths or tables, and the dealers are there to sell. You have many opportunities to comparison shop, and you are also exposed to dealers you might not otherwise meet.

Many stamp societies also take space at shows, because it's a good opportunity to recruit new members. One advantage of signing up with an organization at a stamp show instead of by mail is that instead of reading promotional fliers and other literature about them, you have the opportunity to talk directly with club representatives, to find out what the clubs offer and to find out if a given club is right for you.

At some shows, there will be a temporary United States Postal Service station where you can mail letters and buy stamps. But the biggest attraction of temporary post offices is that they offer special postmarks, usually pictorials. The letters you mail at the show will bear the special postmark, so it's a good way to "dress up" your correspondence. The show sponsors usually sell a special commemorative envelope, which you can adorn with the stamp of your choice and have canceled with the show postmark; then you can take it with you (you don't even have to mail the envelope!) for a special souvenir.

20 PHASIANUS COLCHICUS

JUGOSLAVIJA

M. ZLAMALIK

COURVOISIER S.A.

A colorful stamp from Yugoslavia (or "Jugoslavia," as the Scott Catalogue and some dealers call it) depicting a bird. You could put this into one of many topical collections: Birds, animals, and nature are just three that come to mind.

ENSURING HIGH STANDARDS

Many dealers are members of the American Stamp Dealers Association (ASDA), a group that seeks to maintain and develop high standards of business ethics among stamp dealers. The association's goal is that collectors doing business with its members can rest assured that the firms are reputable and trustworthy.

ASDA membership must be earned. In order to be allowed to join the ASDA, a dealer must have at least four years of professional philatelic experience, pass a thorough background check, *and* agree in writing to abide by the organization's code of ethics. If a member cheats you, that dealer has committed professional suicide.

The second of two 1975 stamps that constitute the first nondenominated stamps in U.S. history (the other is shown on page 65). This religious Christmas stamp will always have a face value of ten cents, but because it doesn't have a printed value it can only be used on letters addressed to U.S. locations.

Ghirlandaio: National Gallery
Christmas US postage

If you send in a self-addressed, stamped, #10 envelope, the ASDA will send you a list of dealers in your area who are ASDA members. This is a double benefit for you: Not only will you have a list of local dealers, you'll know you can rely on them, because they're ASDA members. Another list of dealers available from the ASDA, also for a self-addressed, stamped, #10 envelope, is one sorted by the topics the dealers do business in. The address of the ASDA is 3 School Street, Glen Cove, NY 11542.

You *need* stamp dealers. And they need you. After all, it's very unlikely that you'll find a mint, never-hinged 1947 Centennial of U.S. Stamps souvenir sheet just lying on the sidewalk. And, without a buyer, even the most valuable stamp in the world is nothing more than a bit of paper with some moisture-activated adhesive on the back.

1943: Postal zones, a two-digit number after the town name and before the state ("Flushing 65, NY") are introduced—the precursor to today's ZIP code system.

INVESTING IN STAMPS

UNDER AUTHORITY OF
ROBERT E. HANNEGAN, POSTMASTER GENERAL

100TH ANNIVERSARY
UNITED STATES POSTAGE STAMPS

NEW YORK, N.Y., MAY 17-25, 1947

1962: The first Christmas stamps are issued.

1963: ZIP codes are introduced.

tamp collecting should be for enjoyment. Collect stamps because you *like* them. However, given the right material, people can make handsome profits on stamps. The operative words here are *given the right material.*

The author of this book is a collector, not an investor. He collects because he enjoys collecting. It is understood that some readers of this volume are interested in knowing how to make money off stamps. But this is very subjective information. Clearly, there is no magic formula for collecting for profit. That kind of timely information is beyond the scope of this book. What may be a good investment as this book is being written might not necessarily be a good gamble by the time you read it.

At right is a twenty-four-cent stamp showing George Washington, from the 1861 definitive series. This souvenir sheet (opposite) reproduces the first two U.S. stamps in exact size. It was issued in 1947 on the one hundredth anniversary of the first U.S. stamps, and it's an inexpensive way to add these issues to your collection, as long as you don't mind the fact that the reproductions are in different colors from the originals.

Following the adage, "Give a man a fish, and he eats for a day; teach a man how to fish, and he eats for a lifetime," there *are* some common-sense tips that we *can* give you, which, if used wisely, might enable you to figure out for yourself what might make wise investments.

KNOWING THE MARKET

If you're the only one who knows that a given stamp is worth investing in, you'll have a better chance of getting it cheaper than the next person, and that's the whole idea behind investing. If, in this book, we were to make the following recommendation, Buy stamp X, because it can only go up in value, not only would *you* be buying stamp

X, but so would the collector down the street (and for that matter, so would we). And the dealer, seeing the demand for stamp X, would increase the asking price, so everybody would have to pay more for stamp X than if we had just kept our mouths shut.

Investment Tips In no particular order, here are some tips for investing in stamps:

1. *In and of itself, age has nothing to do with value.* One of the more common misconceptions in any hobby, not just stamp collecting, is that if it's old, it's immensely valuable. The author has gone to many stamp shows and bought envelopes postmarked in the late 1800s for a dollar or less.

To illustrate this point through another hobby, take the example of a coin that was made sometime between the years A.D. 395 and 408. This coin is almost *sixteen hundred years old,* yet this author paid less than $10 for it. So, if you want to buy an old stamp just because it's old, then go right ahead—but keep in mind that the age of an item is *not* an intrinsic factor affecting its value.

2. *Demand is more important than supply.* Rarity by itself means nothing. You can have a collectible of which yours is the only specimen in the whole world, but enough people have to *want* to own it to make its rarity affect its value to collectors.

When the Postal Service issued a pictorial postal card showing the White House in 1989, we obtained five cards with the special "First Day of Issue" cancellation applied in the message area instead of canceling the stamp. And to our knowledge, ours were the only five cards in the whole world where the cancellation was placed in the message area, as opposed to thousands of cards where the "First Day" cancellation actually canceled the stamped portion of the card. Yes, it's definitely *rare*—but on the other hand, the author is the only person who really cares about postmark placement to such an extent that he would request it this way. So, while it *is* rare, the only

1977: The higher rate for domestic airmail is eliminated. By this time most of the mail was being transported by air regardless of whether air service was paid for by the mailer. A separate fee for *international* airmail still exists.

person who wants one already has one. In fact, he has five, so the case could be made that for the amount of potential buyers (one), there is an overabundant supply (five).

One of the most valuable stamps in the world is a 1¢ stamp from British Guiana (now know as Guyana) that was issued in 1851. Only one copy is known to exist. It is in used condition, and it's damaged to boot. This British Guiana stamp is so desirable that in 1980 someone paid $935,000 for it. Yet there are other stamps of which there is only one copy, but are not even close in value to this one. How can that be? From the time its existence was made known to the present, it has acquired a distinguished pedigree—many notable collectors have owned it or tried to (according to legend, King George V of England attempted to buy it), putting this stamp in a class above any other.

A valuable stamp doesn't have to be a world-class rarity that a king could not obtain. It could be one of which mil-

Pair of 1924 five-cent definitives showing Theodore Roosevelt. This is a coil pair, identified as such by the lack of perforations on top or bottom. Coils are collected in pairs of two or more to help show their coil status.

This stamp from the African nation of Ruanda-Urundi (now called Rwanda) would not only fall into a topical collection of animals, but it could also go into a collection of African stamps; of stamps with scientific names of animals; or stamps issued in franc denominations. This ninety-cent stamp (opposite) was issued in 1861. Because of the outbreak of the Civil War, all U.S. stamps issued up until then were invalidated so as to prevent the South from using them, and new stamps had to be issued to replace them.

lions of examples were issued—but if there's a demand for it, its value will go up.

3. *There is no substitute for knowledge,* a point we've made before and we're going to make again. We've already discussed philatelic literature in an earlier chapter, so we'll just put it like this: Collecting stamps without reading about them is like buying a car and not reading the owner's manual.

One book we read when we started out in stamps was a book called *Fun and Profit in Stamp Collecting,* by Herman Herst, Jr. Herst is a longtime stamp dealer who is also well known as a very prolific philatelic writer, and this author highly recommends this book to all those who are interested in investing in stamps. The book was written in 1962, but a revised edition was published in 1988 by Amos Press of Sidney, Ohio. Even if it hadn't been revised, it would still be worth reading. Good advice is never outdated.

OTHER WAYS TO COLLECT

This two-cent stamp was issued in 1894. The value of this cover (opposite) stems from the fact that the postmark is a "fancy cancel"—an obliterator created at the whim of the postmaster. In the days before cancellation devices were standardized, some very imaginative designs were created, and today they are extremely collectible and can greatly increase the value of a stamp. If the stamp were removed from this cover much of the value would be lost. In many cases, stamps on cover are worth more than the same stamp soaked off— when in doubt, keep the whole envelope and consult a dealer or other knowledgeable collector for an expert opinion.

This book has concentrated on stamp collecting as it relates to the acquisition of individual, mint stamps. Which is not to say that's the only way to collect, for it most certainly isn't. There are many other ways to collect—so many that it would require a book many times the size of this one to be able to do justice to each of them. This chapter will discuss some of the them.

As you go out and about in your philatelic career and you come across a specialty that appeals to you, don't let the fact that it wasn't discussed here prevent you from partaking in its joys.

USED STAMPS

Used stamps are stamps that, having served their postal duty, have been canceled to prevent reuse. Some collectors

feel that a stamp isn't truly legitimate unless it *has* been canceled. These collectors say that because stamps were created to serve a given purpose, they're nothing more than glorified labels unless they do serve that purpose.

One advantage of collecting used stamps is that you don't have to be concerned about whether or not the gum on the back is original, since there won't be any. It will have been removed when the stamp was soaked off the envelope. (This allows you to hinge your stamps if that's the method you prefer.)

For the most part, used stamps are less expensive than mint stamps, although there are some instances where this is not so. In these cases, it's probably better to keep the stamp on the original envelope in order to help verify that it actually was used. Fakers have been known to remove the gum from a mint stamp, add a phony cancel,

1978: The United States Postal Service begins copyrighting its stamps and philatelic products. Current American stamps have a copyright notice in the selvage.

and pass it off as a rare used example. Most of the time, though, you won't have to worry about it.

The most desirable used stamps to have are those with a lightly-applied cancel or those that have been just "nicked" by a cancel. The goal is to be able to see the stamp's design clearly despite the cancellation (unless your aim is to collect examples of rare cancels).

Some used stamps are valuable because of the particular cancellation they bear. In the 1800s, many postmasters created their own fancy cancels by whittling a design out of cork or other material, and they'd use them to obliterate the stamp. Such fancy cancels are popular with specialists, so a common used stamp might sell for a significantly higher amount because of a fancy cancel. Individual postmasters' practice of creating their own cancellations has not been permitted for many years.

Except for the cost of fancy cancels, a collection of used stamps will pretty much be an inexpensive endeavor, though one that's not as easy as it seems. Dealers may only have them in collections of packets or mixtures, since recent used stamps are not profitable.

PLATE BLOCKS

A plate block in its most basic form is a block of four stamps that also has the number of the printing plate used to print the stamps on the selvage. It's not as simple as that, though; it really depends on the way a stamp was printed.

Stamps printed by the flat-plate method must be collected in blocks of six, not four. On these, the plate number must be in the center of the selvage, not on the left or right sides.

On multicolored stamps, for which each color has its own plate number (the printing process uses a new plate for each color), the plate block can have as many as ten—or even twenty—stamps. Some stamps have what are known as floating plate numbers; in cases of multicolored

1983: Express Mail next-day service begins. A special $9.35 stamp, valid on all mail matter, is issued to meet the rate. It is the highest face value American postage stamp issued up to this point.

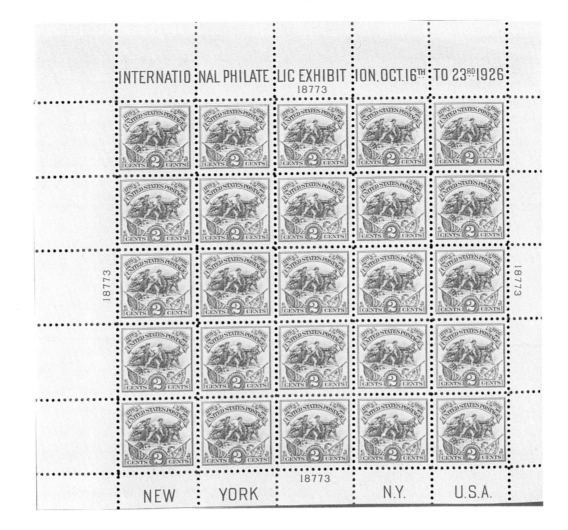

stamps, it means almost a half a sheet makes up the plate block.

Collectors rebel at the cost of buying so many stamps. In an attempt to reduce the expense (and regain customers), the Postal Service has changed the plate-numbering system from cumulatively numbering each plate (for example, 20413, 20414, and so on), to giving each color a single-digit number. Thus a current plate block for a multicolored stamp might have plate number 11111, but each "1" would be a different color.

A specialized stamp catalog can usually tell you how many stamps are required for a plate block on a stamp-by-stamp basis.

The first U.S. souvenir sheet was issued in 1926. It consisted of a miniature sheet of twenty-five of a then-current commemorative (the 1926 150th Anniversary of the Battle of White Plains issue) with a special inscription in the selvage: "INTERNATIONAL PHILATELIC EXHIBITION OCT 18th TO 23rd 1926" on top, "NEW YORK N.Y. U.S.A." on the bottom.

The first U.S. self-adhesive stamp was issued in 1974, a Christmas issue showing the dove-shaped weather vane atop Mount Vernon. Most of these stamps have since become discolored because of the kind of adhesive used on the back. Self-adhesive stamps were not tried again by the U.S. until 1989, when an experimental booklet of eighteen was issued in fifteen test cities. Experimental self-adhesive stamps were also issued in 1990—in currency-shaped sheets of twelve, for sale through ATMs in Seattle.

BOOKLETS

A stamp booklet allows you to keep your stamps in an easy-to-carry format. The advantage of booklets for the postal customer is that there is no worry about loose stamps, since the stamps remain in the book until needed, and in the meantime they're protected by the cover.

Each page of a booklet is called a *pane,* and an unopened booklet is called an *unexploded booklet.* A stamp from a booklet has one or two straight edges, but that doesn't make them the same as imperforate stamps.

For many years, definitives were used to make up booklets. This is still the case, but the Postal Service also issues pictorial stamps in booklet form only. In 1986, separate booklets were issued honoring stamp collecting and fish. Other topics issued in booklets by the United States have been animals, cars, special-message stamps ("Happy Birthday," "Thinking of You," "Best Wishes," for example), steamboats, classic automobiles, lighthouses, and so on.

PLATE-NUMBER COILS

One of the more recent collecting specialties is plate-number coils. Coil stamps are sold in rolls (coil stamps are straight on two sides, usually on the top and bottom), and at the bottom there is a little number indicating the plate it was printed on.

The Postal Service started putting plate numbers on the coil stamps in 1981. Collectors usually save plate-number coils in strips of three, or strips of five, with the plate-number stamp being in the middle. Some plate numbers are more valuable than others, and stamps that were issued in the 1980s, can be worth a *lot* of money—perhaps even *thousands* of dollars!

Plate-number coil collecting is still a relatively new phase of stamp collecting, so the beginner should probably just stick to saving any plate-number singles that happen to come along on incoming mail.

COVERS

A cover is any kind of an envelope that has passed through the mail. It can have a canceled stamp on it, or no stamp, or a meter impression, or a permit imprint. The envelopes you receive in the mail are covers. They're called covers because they cover, or conceal, the message contained within.

If you come across a stamp in your mail that you'd like, don't take if off the envelope immediately. Sometimes the whole envelope can be worth more than the used stamp alone because of the postmark. The best thing is to show the stamp and cover to a dealer, who can give you

1971: The United States Post Office Department, a branch of government, is abolished. It is replaced by the United States Postal Service, a semigovernmental organization.

1974: First self-adhesive stamp is issued.

1975: First nondenominated stamps are issued.

an opinion on whether to take the stamp off or save the whole cover.

You can save covers for many reasons, to keep an example of a particular postal rate or usage or to have a cover postmarked on your birthday, for instance.

FIRST DAY COVERS

A First Day Cover is similar to a regular cover, except that the stamp on that envelope has the postmark of the first day the stamp was put on sale.

Most every United States stamp is first put on sale in one city, usually one that somehow relates to the subject. No other city is allowed to sell that stamp on the First Day—but on the next day, every post office nationwide may put the stamp up for sale.

There are two ways that you can service your own First Day Covers—before the First Day, send a check or money order made payable to the postmaster of the First Day city, enclose an *un*stamped self-addressed envelope, and mail it to the postmaster of the First Day city. The other method, and the one that the Postal Service prefers, is that you buy the stamp yourself (*after* the first day of issue), affix it to your self-addressed envelope, and then mail it to the First Day city—customer-affixed covers will get preferential service.

It may seem strange to buy the stamp yourself after the First Day and then receive a postmark dated the First Day, when you didn't even get the stamp until the day after. But that's a result of the growing popularity of First Day Covers. In 1969, almost *9 million* First Day Covers were serviced for the 10¢ airmail stamp commemorating the first man on the moon.

The earliest First Day Covers were created by chance. A postal customer who needed to mail a letter went to the post office and bought a stamp that happend to be coming out that day, put it on the envelope, and mailed it, and it received a First Day dated postmark.

1989: First United States picture postal card is issued. It is a picture postcard with a stamp printed on the card, which the Postal Service calls the EXTRAordinary View Card. The 15¢ card sells for 50¢.

A First Day Cover of the nine-cent National Parks issue of 1934 (top), depicting Mt. Rockwell and Two Medicine Lake in Glacier National Park, Montana. The illustration on the left-hand part of the envelope is called a cachet, and is privately made. (Collecting First Day Covers by cachetmaker is a very popular specialty of First Day Cover collectors.) The postmark used on this cover is the ordinary working-day cancellation, but First Day Covers were getting so popular that by 1937 a special cancel with the inscription ''First Day of Issue'' was put into use. This 1976 prestamped envelope (above) was part of a five-envelope 1975-1976 Bicentennial era series. This envelope salutes the American craftsman, and the rocking chair illustration is part of the design—not a privately produced cachet.

Bicentennial Era   The American Craftsman

In the 1920s, collectors began sending addressed envelopes and money to First Day postmasters, asking them to affix the new stamp and cancel it with a postmark dated the First Day—postmasters accommodated them, because it was easier to do that than write back and explain that they couldn't. Eventually, the Post Office Department, precursor of the United States Postal Service, became more cooperative. The department realized that First Day Covers were profitable, and in 1937, it began using the special cancellation "First Day of Issue." For stamps issued prior to that date, you have to know what the First Day was in order to make sure a given cover actually is a First Day Cover. You can find this information in stamp catalogs.

First Day Cover collectors prefer their covers unaddressed. Those who send away for them usually write their address on a removable label, and when the First Day Covers arrive, they remove the label. They also prefer to have a cachet on the envelope. A cachet is a design of some kind that helps explain the significance of the envelope, and it can be printed or drawn by hand. The cachet can have a significant influence on the value of a First Day Cover. Two First Day Covers with the same stamp, but different cachets can vary significantly in worth.

"Serious" philatelists do not look favorably upon First Day Covers, seeing them as nothing more than philatelic souvenirs. It is true that a lot of attention is focused on the cachet, and cachets do not move the mail. But First Day Covers are fun to collect, and if you have some artistic talent, you might decide to become a cachet maker yourself. About the best endorsement we can give First Day Covers is that we collect them and enjoy them very much.

As we said at the beginning of this chapter, these are just a few of the many other ways you can collect. Don't be surprised if you pick up a catalog or a philatelic newspaper and discover something not discussed here; the world of stamp collecting is so vast that we couldn't even begin to list all the possibilities.

There are so many stamps to collect, so many rarities to learn about, so many new innovations the Postal Service is experimenting with, that it can *never* be the end. Stamp collecting is a wholesome, worthwhile hobby that can last a lifetime.

Who knows? Perhaps you may be the next William T. Robey. In 1918, Robey went to a Washington, D.C., post office, and bought a sheet of airmail stamps only to find that the plane was upside-down. According to legend, Robey asked the window clerk if there were any more like that, but when the clerk tried to take back the stamps and replace them with normally printed ones, Robey refused. (Postal clerks are not allowed to *knowingly* sell any error stamps, even if they're not getting anything out of it, so the unknown clerk who sold the stamps to Robey

1989: First United States postal item with a hologram is issued, a 25¢ prestamped envelope with a space-station design in the hologram.

This is the most famous of all U.S. stamps—the one with the upside down plane. Known as the "inverted Jenny," the error came about as a result of the sheet being fed the wrong way into the press during the printing process. One hundred of these are known to exist; it's speculated that four hundred were printed, but the other three hundred have never turned up and are presumed to have been caught and destroyed. The error was discovered in Washington, D.C. by collector William T. Robey on May 13, 1918—the stamp's first day of issue.

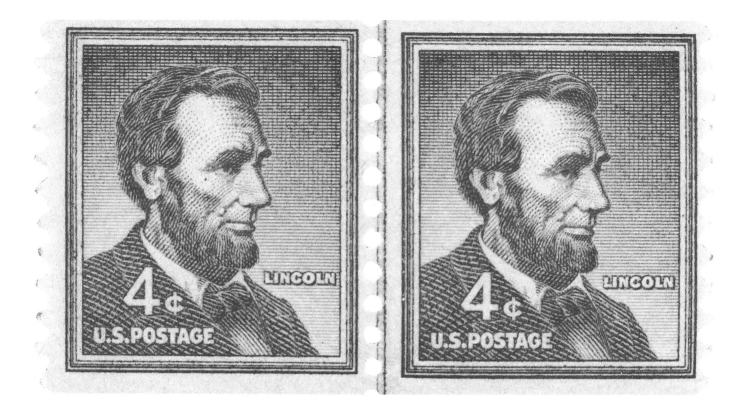

1990: First plastic stamps are issued, a sheet of twelve 25¢ stamps, designed to be sold through ATM machines. The self-adhesive stamps are issued in Seattle, Washington, on an experimental basis.

1990: The first postage stamp is 150 years old.

was just doing his job.) Even postal inspectors couldn't convince Robey to return the error sheet. Today, one of these stamps, known as the Inverted Jenny because Jenny is the name of the type of plane depicted on the stamp, sells for well into six figures at auction, making it one of the most valuable American stamps. One day *you* might discover an error, and if you're lucky you could make some good money off of it.

But the main thing, as we've tried to highlight throughout the course of this book, is to have some fun and enjoy yourself with your stamp collection. Your stamp collection is there for *you* to enjoy, and if someone else doesn't like it, that's not your problem. Don't buy stamps you don't particularly care about just to impress someone else. By the same token, if you like a country or topic that another collector abhors, that doesn't mean *you* have to stop collecting it.

This three-cent stamp, of which a used pair is shown, was issued in 1851 as part of only the second definitive series of U.S. postage stamps. A coil line pair of the 1958 Abraham Lincoln four-cent definitive (opposite). A coil line pair is a pair of coil stamps which has a line between the stamps— from the space where ink collects between the sections of different printing plates.

And don't worry if you find that some people scoff at you at first for asking questions that seem stupid to them. Of course they seem stupid to them; they've been collecting for years, so what you're asking is old hat. Don't let it bother you, though, and *never* feel intimidated if you have to ask a "stupid" question: It's *not* a stupid question if you don't know the answer to it.

Besides, at some time or another everyone was a beginner. Even the guy who wrote this book was once a beginner, so why should you feel any different?

Good luck, and happy collecting!

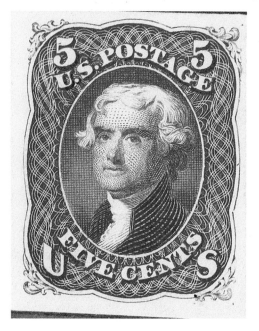

This five-cent stamp was issued in 1861.

PHILATELIC SOCIETIES

Why should you join a philatelic society? For one thing, most (if not all) societies regularly publish a journal in which you can find detailed articles that sometimes represent years of research, and other informative writings concerning what you like to collect. Society journals are valuable assets in this regard.

Many organizations have local branches, and by attending meetings you can also meet people who are interested in the same thing you are. Who knows better than a collector what it's like to be one?

A list of national philatelic societies follows. Because of space limitations, we could not list each and every organization that's around. Groups are listed in alphabetical order. Many organizations are nonprofit, and philatelic courtesy requires those who make inquiries through the mail to enclose a stamped, self-addressed envelope along with any request. After all, it's not fair for society members to spend their dues to answer your inquiry.

Aerophilatelic Federation of
the Americas
Basle Burrell
P.O. Box 1239
Elgin, IL 60121

American Air Mail Society
102 Arbor Road
Cinnaminson, NJ 08077

American First Day Cover
Society
Mrs. Monte Eiserman
14359 Chadbourne
Houston, TX 77079

American Philatelic Congress
Dr. Russell Skavaril
222 East Torrence Road
Columbus, OH 43214

American Philatelic Society
P.O. Box 8000
State College, PA 16803

American Plate Number
Single Society
Box 375
Glen Echo, MD 20812

American Society for
Philatelic Pages and Panels
Gerland Blankenship
P.O. Box 4765
Crosby, TX 77532

American Topical Association
Donald Smith
P.O. Box 630
Johnstown, PA 15907

Booklet Collectors Club
1016 East El Camino Real
No. 107
Sunnyvale, CA 94087

Bureau Issues Association/
United States Stamp Society
George Godin
P.O. Box 1047
Belleville, IL 62223

Civil Censorship Study Group
Dann Mayo
P.O. Box 20837
Indianapolis, IN 46220

Errors, Freaks and Oddities
    Collectors Club
James McDevitt
1903 Village Road
West Norwood, MA 02062

Essay-Proof Society
Barbara Mueller
225 South Fischer Avenue
Jefferson, WI 53549

Fine Arts Philatelists
Dr. Tom Ullrich
7502 East 80 Street
Indianapolis, IN 46256

Gay and Lesbian History on
    Stamps Club
Ed Centeno
P.O. Box 3940
Hartford, CT 06103

International Philatelic Golf
    Society
Kevin Hadlock
447 Skyline Drive
Orange, CT 06477

International Society of Reply
    Coupon Collectors
Dr. Allan Hauck
P.O. Box 165
Somers, WI 53171

Judaica Historical Philatelic
    Society
Sam Simon
80 Bruce Avenue
Yonkers, NY 10705

Mailer's Postmark Permit
    Club
Florence Sugarberg
P.O. Box 5793
Akron, OH 44372

Maritime Postmark Society
Fred McGary
P.O. Box 1264
Absecon, NJ 08201

Maximum Card Study Unit
Ed Cramer
4702 Main Street
Skokie, IL 60076

Metropolitan Airpost Society
E. Lettick
31 Orangewood West
Derby, CT 06418

Mobile Post Office Society
Andrew Koval
P.O. Box 502
Bedford Park, IL 60499

The Philatelic Foundation
21 East 40th Street
New York, NY 10016

Plate Number Coil Collectors
    Club (PNC³)
Eric Russow
P.O. Box 7386
Des Moines, IA 50309

Postal History Society
Kalman V. Illyefalvi
8207 Daren Court
Pikesville, MD 21208

Postal History Foundation
P.O. Box 40725
Tucson, Arizona 85717

Postmark Collectors Club
Wilma Hinrichs
4200 S.E. Indianola Road
Des Moines, IA 50320

Postal Order Society
Jack Harwood
P.O. Box 32015
Midtown Station
Sarasota, FL 34239

Czeslaw Slania Study Group
Edith Ann Malson
P.O. Box 1382
Milwaukee, WI 53201

Stamps on Stamps Centenary
    Unit
Bunny Kaplan
855 Stonehenge Road
Cherry Hill, NJ 08003

U.S. 1869 Pictorial Research
    Associates
William Wickert
3348 Club House Road
Virginia Beach, VA 23452

U.S. Philatelic Classics
    Society
Michael O'Reilly
P.O. Box 1131
Huntsville, AL 35807

United Postal Stationery
    Society
UPSS Central Office
P.O. Box 48
Redlands, CA 92373

Universal Postal Union
    Collectors
Bob Malch
P.O. Box 607117
Orlando, FL 32860

Zeppelin Collectors Club
Cheryl Ganz
P.O. Box 3843
Chicago, IL 60690

This Russian stamp is canceled to order (CTO). CTOs are created by some postal administrations in order to create product they can sell at a discount to dealers. Unlike legitimately used stamps, CTOs are generally canceled whole sheets at a time, and they still have the gum on the back. CTOs are practically worthless, so if you ever come across a letter franked with a stamp from a country known to issue CTOs you're better off saving the whole envelope as proof that the stamp served its postal duty.

POSTAL ADMINISTRATIONS

Throughout this book, the focus has been on collecting United States stamps. Of course, the world is more than the United States, and lots of collectors also save the stamps of other nations. Dealers can sell you older issues, but one way of getting new issues is to write directly to the postal administration of the country that interests you.

One disadvantage of dealing directly with foreign countries is having to worry about foreign exchange. Many countries have authorized agents in the United States to represent them in selling their new issues. Be aware, however, that some American representatives set their own minimums, which may or may not coincide with the way you collect. The Unicover World Trade Corporation of Cheyenne, Wyoming, which represents a number of countries, has a minimum purchase requirement of four stamps, *before* you can buy anything else, which means even if you want only a First Day Cover, you still have to buy four stamps before they will sell you one.

In this section, local addresses are listed for each country. If a country has an American representative, that address is listed as well, so in those cases you can write either to the country or its American representative.

Aitutaki
Aitutaki Post Office
Cook Islands
South Pacific Ocean

Aland
Mariehamns Postkontor
Filateliservicen
PO 100
22101 Mariehamn
Finland

U.S. Representative:
Unicover World Trade
    Corporation
Finland Stamp Agency in
    North America
One Unicover Center
Cheyenne, WY 82008

Algeria
Receveur Principal Des Postes
Alger R.P.
Algeria

Anguilla
The Postmaster
General Post Office
The Valley
Anguilla, West Indies

Antigua-Barbuda
Philatelic Bureau
Barbuda Post Office
Codrington, Barbuda
West Indies (Via Antigua)

U.S. Representative:
Inter-Governmental Philatelic
    Corporation

460 West 34th Street
New York, NY 10001

Argentina
Seccion Filatelia
Correo Central Local 55
1000 Buenos Aires, Argentina

Aruba
Aruba Philatelic Service
Post Office
Oranjestad, Aruba

Ascension
Postmaster
Jamestown
St. Helena, South Atlantic

Australia
Australian Philatelic Bureau
GPO Box 9988
Melbourne, Victoria 3001
Australia

U.S. Representative:
Unicover World Trade
　Corporation
Australian Stamp Agency in
　North America
One Unicover Center
Cheyenne, WY 82008

Austria
Osterreichische Post
Briefmarkenversandstelle
A-1211 Vienna, Austria

U.S. Representative:
Inter-Governmental Philatelic
　Corporation
460 West 34th Street
New York, NY 10001

Bahamas
Postmaster General
GPO
P.O. Box N8302
Nassau, Bahamas

Bangladesh
Office of the Director General
Bangladesh Post Office
Dacca 1000, Bangladesh

Barbados
Philatelic Bureau
GPO
Bridgetown, Barbados,
West Indies

Belgium
Regie des Postes
Division 1.1.4.2.
Service des Collectionneurs
Centre Monnaie
1000 Brussels, Belgium

Bermuda
Bermuda Philatelic Bureau
GPO
Hamilton, HMPM, Bermuda

Bhutan
Dy. Director
Philatelic Bureau
GPO
Thimphu, Bhutan

U.S. Representative:
Inter-Governmental Philatelic
　Corporation
460 West 34th Street
New York, NY 10001

Botswana
Department of Postal Service
Philatelic Bureau

Box 100
Gaborone, Botswana

U.S. Representative:
Inter-Governmental Philatelic
　Corporation
460 West 34th Street
New York, NY 10001

Brazil
ECT, Accessoria Filatelica,
　SCS
Quadra 4, Bloco A, No. 230
Edificia Apolo, 7⁰ Andar
Brasilia, DF, Brazil

U.S. Representative
Unicover World Trade
　Corporation
Brazil Stamp Agency in
　North America
One Unicover Center
Cheyenne, WY 82008

British Antarctic Territory
Postmaster for British
　Antarctic Territory
c/o GPO
Port Stanley, Falkland Islands

British Virgin Islands
The Postmaster
Philatelic Bureau
Road Town
Tortola, British Virgin Islands

U.S. Representative
Inter-Governmental Philatelic
　Corporation
460 West 34th Street
New York, NY 10001

Canada

National Philatelic Centre
Canada Post Corporation
Antigonish, NS
B2G 2R8, Canada

U.S. Representative
Unicover World Trade
   Corporation
Canada Post Stamp Service in
   the United States
One Unicover Center
Cheyenne, WY 82008

Cayman Islands

Postmaster General
Philatelic Bureau
GPO, Georgetown
Grand Cayman
Cayman Islands
British West Indies

Chile

Empresa de Correos de Chile
Servicio Filatelico
Moneda 1155
Santiago, Chile

U.S. Representative:
Unicover Trade Corporation
One Unicover Center
Cheyenne, WY 82008

China

China National Philatelic
Corporation
He Ping Men
Beijing, China

U.S. Representative:
Unicover World Trade
   Corporation
China Stamp Agency in
   North America
One Unicover Center
Cheyenne, WY 82008

Republic of China (Taiwan)

Philatelic Department
Directorate General of Posts
Taipei 10603
Taiwan, Republic of China

U.S. Representative:
World Wide Philatelic Agency
2031 Carolina Place
Fort Mill, SC 29715

Christmas Island

Philatelic Bureau
Christmas Island
Indian Ocean 6798

Colombia

Oficina Filatelica
Administracion Postal
   Nacional
Oficina 209
Edificio Murillo Toro
Bogota 1, Colombia

Czechoslovakia

Artia Foreign Trade
   Corporation
Box 790
Prague 1, Czechoslovakia

Denmark

Postens Frimaerkecenter
Vesterbrogade 67
DK 1620 Copenhagen V,
Denmark

U.S. Representative:
Nordica Inc.
Box 284
Old Bethpage, NY 11804

Egypt

Postal Organization Philatelic
   Office
Cairo, Arab Republic of Egypt

Ethiopia

Ethiopian Postal Service
Philatelic Section
Box 1112
Addis Ababa, Ethiopia

U.S. Representative:
Inter-Governmental Philatelic
   Corporation
460 West 34th Street
New York, NY 10001

Fiji

Philatelic Bureau
Box 100
Suva, Fiji

Finland

Posts and Telecommunications
   of Finland
Philatelic Center
Box 654 (Salomonkatu 1)
SF-00101 Helsinki, Finland

U.S. Representative:
Unicover World Trade
   Corporation
Finland Stamp Agency in
   North America
One Unicover Center
Cheyenne, WY 82008

France

Service Philatelique De La
   Poste
18 rue Francois Bonvin
F-75758, Paris, Codex 15,
France

U.S. Representative:
Unicover World Trade
   Corporation
French Stamp Agency in
   North America
One Unicover Center
Cheyenne, WY 82008

West Germany
Versandstelle fur
  Postwertzeichen
Sammler—Service der Poste
Box 20 00
6000 Frankfurt 1
Federal Republic of Germany

U.S. Representative:
Interpost
Box 378
Malverne, NY 11565

Gibraltar
Gibraltar Post Office
Philatelic Bureau
Box 5662, Gibraltar

U.S. Representative:
Inter-Governmental Philatelic
  Corporation
460 West 34th Street
New York, NY 10001

United Kingdom
British Philatelic Bureau
20 Brandon Street
Edinburgh EH3 5TT, Scotland

U.S. Representative:
Interpost
Box 378
Malverne, NY 11565

Greece
Greek Post Office
Philatelic Service
100 Aeolou Street
GR-101 88, Athens, Greece

U.S. Representative:
Interpost
Box 378
Malverne, NY 11565

Guyana
Guyana Post Office
  Corporation
Robb Street
Georgetown, Guyana

Hong Kong
Hong Kong Post Office
Philatelic Bureau
GPO 2, Connaught Place
Hong Kong

U.S. Representative:
Interpost
Box 378
Malverne, NY 11565

India
Philatelic Bureau
GPO
Bombay 400001, India

U.S. Representative:
Inter-Governmental Philatelic
  Corporation
460 West 34th Street
New York, NY 10001

Ireland
The Controller
Philatelic Bureau
GPO
Dublin 1, Ireland

U.S. Representative:
Interpost
Box 378
Malverne, NY 11565

Israel
Postal Authority Philatelic
  Service
12 Jerusalem Boulevard
61 080 Tel Aviv, Yafo, Israel

U.S. Representative:
Unicover World Trade
  Corporation
Israel Stamp Agency in
  North America
One Unicover Center
Cheyenne, WY 82008

Italy
Ufficio Principale Filatelico
Via Mario de'Fiori, 103/A
00187 Rome, Italy

Japan
Philatelic Section
CPO Box 888
Tokyo 100–91, Japan

Kenya
Philatelic Bureau
Box 30368
Nairobi, Kenya

U.S. Representative:
Inter-Governmental Philatelic
  Corporation
460 West 34th Street
New York, NY 10001

Liechtenstein
Official Philatelic Service
FL-9490 Vaduz
Principality of Liechtenstein

Luxembourg
Direction des Postes
Office des Timbres
L-2020, Luxembourg
Grand Duchy of Luxembourg

Mexico
Grencia de Servicio Filatelico
San Antonio Abad 130–7°
  Piso, Col. Transito
06820 Mexico D.F., Mexico

Monaco
Office des Emissions
  de Timbres-Postes
Department de Finances
Principality of Monaco

U.S. Representative:
Unicover World Trade
  Corporation
Stamp Agency of the
  Principality of Monaco
  in North America
One Unicover Center
Cheyenne, WY 82008

Morocco
Ministere des PTT
Division Postale
Rabat, Morocco

Myanmar
(formerly **Burma**)
Myanmar Export Import
  Corporation
Export Division, Philatelic
  Section
Yangou, Myanmar

Netherlands
Netherlands Post Office
  Philatelic Service
Box 30051
9700 RN Groningen
Netherlands

U.S. Representative:
World Wide Philatelic Agency
2031 Carolina Place
Fort Mill, SC 29715

New Zealand
Philatelic Bureau
110 Victoria Avenue
Private Bag
Wanganui, New Zealand

U.S. Representative:
Unicover World Trade
  Corporation
New Zealand Stamp Agency
  in North America
One Unicover Center
Cheyenne, WY 82008

Nigeria
Nigerian Philatelic Service
GPO
Tinubu Street
P.M.B. 12647
Lagos, Nigeria

Norway:
Norwegian Post Philatelic
  Bureau
Box 3770
Gamlebyen
N-0135 Oslo 1, Norway

Pakistan
Pakistan Philatelic Bureau
GPO
Karachi, Pakistan

Panama
Direccion General de Correos
  y Telecomunicaciones
Departmento de Filatelia
Apartado 3421
Panama 1, Panama

Philippines
Stamp and Philatelic Section
Postal Services Office
Liwasang Bonifacio
1000 Manila, Philippines

Poland
Ars Polona
Box 1001
00–222 Warsaw, Poland

Portugal
Direccao de Relacoes
  Internacionals e Filatelia
Av. Casal Robeiro 2802⁰
1096 Lisbon Codex, Portugal

U.S. Representative:
Interpost
Box 378
Malverne, NY 11565

Romania
Rompresfilatelia
Calea Grivitei 64166
Bucharest, Romania

Singapore
Philatelic Bureau
Postal Services Group
Telecoms
31 Exeter Road 25–00
Comcentre, Singapore 0923
Republic of Singapore

U.S. Representative:
Inter-Governmental Philatelic
  Corporation
460 West 34th Street
New York, NY 10001

South Korea
Korean Philatelic Center
CPO Box 5122
Seoul 100–651
Republic of Korea

U.S. Representative:
Kent Research Stamp
Company
201 Mill Road, Box 86
Hewlett, NY 11557

Spain
Direccion General de Correos
  e Telegrafos
Seccion De Filatelia
Palacio de Comunicaciones
28070 Madrid, Spain

Sri Lanka
Philatelic Bureau
Department of Posts
4th Floor, Ceylinco House
Colombo 1, Sri Lanka

U.S. Representative:
Inter-Governmental Philatelic
  Corporation
460 West 34th Street
New York, NY 10001

Sweden
PFA Swedish Stamps
S-1645 88
Kista, Sweden

U.S. Representative:
Unicover World Trade
  Corporation
Sweden Stamp Agency
  in North America
One Unicover Center
Cheyenne, WY 82008

Switzerland
Philatelic Service PTT
Zeughausgasse 19
CH-3030 Bern, Switzerland

Thailand
Chief of Philatelic Promotion
  Section
The Communications
  Authority of Thailand
Chaengwattana Road
Laksi, Bangkok 10002,
Thailand

Togo
Direction General des Postes
  et Communications
Direction des Services Postaux
  et Financiers
Lome, Togo

U.S. Representative:
Inter-Governmental Philatelic

Corporation
460 West 34th Street
New York, NY 10001

Turkey
PTT Filateli Servisi
P.K. 900 Ulus
TR-06045, Ankara, Turkey

U.S. Representative:
Inter-Governmental Philatelic
  Corporation
460 West 34th Street
New York, NY 10001

Turks and Caicos Islands
Philatelic Bureau
Grand Turk
Turks and Caicos Islands
West Indies

U.S. Representative:
Inter-Governmental Philatelic
  Corporation
460 West 34th Street
New York, NY 10001

Uganda
Uganda Posts and
  Telecommunications
  Corporation
Department of Posts
Stamps Bureau
Box 7106
Kampala, Uganda

U.S. Representative:
Inter-Governmental Philatelic
  Corporation
460 West 34th Street
New York, NY 10001

Union of Soviet Socialist Republics (USSR)
U.S. Representative:
Unicover World Trade
  Corporation

USSR Stamp Service
  in North America
One Unicover Center
Cheyenne, WY 82008

United States of America
United States Postal Service
Philatelic Sales Division
Box 449997
Kansas City, MO 64144-9997

Vatican City
Ufficio Filatelico
  del Governatorato
Vatican City

Venezuela
Instituto Postal Telegrafico
  de Venezuela
Oficina Filatelica Nacional
Apartado 4080
Caracas, 1010-A, Venezuela

Western Samoa
Supervisor, Philatelic Bureau
GPO
Apia, Western Samoa
South Pacific

Yugoslavia
U.S. Representative:
Unicover World Trade
  Corporation
Yugoslavia Stamp Service
  in North America
One Unicover Center
Cheyenne, WY 82008

Zimbabwe
Posts and Telecommunication
  Corporation
Philatelic Bureau
Box 4220
Harare, Zimbabwe

INDEX

A

Aerogrammes, 27, *35*
Age and value, 92
Airmail, 15, 22, *30*, 54
  domestic, 20, 21, 92
  international, 11, 20, *35*, 92
  special delivery, *23*
Aitutaki, postal administration,
  112
Aland, postal administration, 112
Albums, 69–74
  blank, 70–71, *70*
  printed, *68*, 69–70, *69*
Algeria, postal administration, 112
American Philatelic Society, 45
American Stamp Dealers Association
  (ASDA), 85, 86
Anguilla, postal administration, 112
Antigua-Barbuda, postal administration,
  112
Approvals, 41–42
Argentina, postal administration, 113
Aruba, postal administration, 113
Ascension, postal administration, 113
Auctions, 42–43, 45, 46
Australia, postal administration, 113
Austria, postal administration, 113
Automated teller machines, 15, 46,
  108

B

Bahamas, postal administration, 113
Bangladesh, postal administration,
  113
Barbados, postal administration, 113
Belgium, postal administration, 113
Bermuda, postal administration, 113
Bhutan, postal administration, 113
Bicentennial series, *105*
Booklets, 9, 24, 102–103
  panes, *14*, 24, *82*, 102
  unexploded, 24, 102
Botswana, postal administration, 113
Bourse, 85
Brazil, postal administration, 113
British Antarctic Territory, postal
  administration, 113
British Virgin Islands, postal
  administration, 113
Bureau of Engraving and Printing
  (BEP), 15
Burma, postal administration, 116

C

Cachet, 106
Canada, 22–24
  postal administration, 114
Cancellations, 12
  fake, 99
  fancy, 80, *98*, 100
  "First Day of Issue," 81, 92, 105
  light, 100
  "nicked," 100
  rare, 100
  special, 32, 105
Cancelled-to-order (CTO), *112*
Catalog
  auction, 42
  Facit, 56
  Michel, 56
  Scott, 52–53, *52*, 54
  specialized, 53, 100
  Stanley Gibbons, 54, 56
  value, 40–41
  Yvert and Ceres, 56
  Zumstein, 56
Cayman Islands, postal
  administration, 114
Certified mail, 18, 23, 54, *54*
Chile, postal administration, 114
China, postal administration, 114
Christmas Island, postal administration,
  114
Christmas seals, 53
Citizens' Stamp Advisory Committee
  (CSAC), 31
Clubs, 85
Coils, 9, 24, *25*
  line pair, *109*
  pair, *93*
  plate number, 103
Colombia, postal administration, 114
Columbus, Christopher, *33*, 47
Commemoratives, 13, 15, 18–19, *30*,
  33, *47*, 54, 56, 72, *101*
Counterfeiting, 75
Country of issue, *11*
Covers, 10, *98*, 103–104
  cachet, 106
  First Day, *81*, 104–106, *105*
  ship-to-shore catapult, *51*
  stampless, *12*, *44*
Czechoslovakia, postal administration,
  114

D

Dealers, 41–42, 80–87
Definitives, 19, *93*, 102, *109*
Demand, supply and, 92–94
Denmark, postal administration, 114
Domestic mail, 11, 20, 21
Domestic Mail Manual, 55

E

Egypt, postal administration, 114
Engraving, 28
  secret, 76
Envelopes. *See also* Covers.
  commemorative, 85
  prestamped, 13, 15, 27, 46, 106
Ethiopia, postal administration, 115
Exhibitions, 85
Express mail, 15, 20, *21*, 22, 100
EXTRAordinary cards, 15, 104

F

Facit catalog, 56
Falkland Islands, postal administration,
  115
Fiji, postal administration, 115
Finland, postal administration, 115
France, postal administration, 115
Franklin, Benjamin, *14*, *26*, *40–41*,
  90
Fun and Profit in Stamp Collecting
  (Herst), 94

G

Gibraltar, postal administration, 115
Graf Zeppelin series, *62–63*
Grant, Ulysses S., *38–39*
Greece, postal administration, 115
Gum, 72, 99
Guyana, postal administration, 115

H

Handstamping, *44*
Herst, Jr., Herman, 94
Hinges, 72
Holograms, 46, 106
Hong Kong, postal administration,
  115